THE
PERFECT FIT

The Perfect Fit: Creating and Altering Basic Sewing Patterns for Tops, Sleeves, Skirts, and Pants

Teresa Gilewska

Project editor: Maggie Yates
Project manager: Lisa Brazieal
Marketing coordinator: Katie Walker
Copyeditor: Maggie Yates
Proofreader: Patricia J. Pane
Graphic Design and Layout: Nord Compo
Layout production: Kim Scott, Bumpy Design
Cover design and production: Kim Scott, Bumpy Design

ISBN: 979-8-88814-148-9
1st Edition (1st printing, March 2024)

Original French title: Les patrons de base sur mesure
© 2019, Éditions Eyrolles, Paris, France

Translation Copyright © 2024 Rocky Nook, Inc.
All illustrations in this work are by the author, with the exception of the following:
Tape measure (p. 187): © studiovin/Shutterstock
Colored pencils (p. 187): © Akura Yochi/Shutterstock
Scissors (p. 187): © Brent Hofacker/Shutterstock
Thread clippers (p. 187): © Passakom sakulphan/Shutterstock
Pins (p. 187): © Olga Popova/Shutterstock

Rocky Nook Inc.
1010 B Street, Suite 350
San Rafael, CA 94901
USA
www.rockynook.com

Distributed in the UK and Europe by Publishers Group UK

Distributed in the U.S. and all other territories by Publishers Group West

Library of Congress Control Number: 2023945249

Printed in China

The

PERFECT
FIT

Creating and Altering
Basic Sewing Patterns for
Tops, Sleeves, Skirts, and Pants

Teresa Gilewska

rockynook

CONTENTS

4

FOREWORD

The idea of writing this book emerged gradually, starting in 2014, the year I founded the Fashion Training Center (*Centre de formation de mode*) in Colmar. Over the following three years, I had the opportunity to interact with an audience that was different from the young students I'd had in my professional and vocational courses (for the French CAP and BP certifications); this was a broader audience made up of people who expressed a clear interest in creating made-to-measure patterns and who convinced me of the need for a book on the subject for the general public.

Thanks to this teaching experience, I was able to collect a number of questions, observations, and reflections from my students that gave me the chance to see what people find easy to learn, and which issues are more complex in learning how to sew, and—more particularly—how to create patterns. The book that you have in your hands now is a result of these experiences. Whether you want to learn how to create patterns for professional purposes or for your own personal use, in these pages you will find a tried-and-true learning method. All of my students, whether beginners or advanced, have learned, each at their own pace, to create their own patterns.

This book approaches the construction of basic patterns according to the method that I use in the courses that I teach: the presentation, the description, and the order of the steps for each of the elements (bodice, sleeve, skirt, and pants) have been carefully thought through, then scrupulously applied with my students. You will find very detailed and precise explanations that will allow you to understand the role and the importance of each line that you draw and the methodical sequence of the steps, which will allow you to make quick and solid progress. Learning to create made-to-measure patterns must proceed according to a definite logic: to progress, it is very important to understand what you are doing at each step along the way.

I want to express my sincere thanks to my students at the Fashion Training Center from 2014 through 2016 for their participation in writing about the complex subjects covered in this work. Their comments, suggestions, and opinions and the designs that they produced were very valuable to me.

Teresa Gilewska

GENERAL CONCEPTS

The technique for drafting a basic pattern using individual measurements is no different from the technique used to create a pattern from standard measurements. The difference between the two processes is that in the case of individual measurements, we need to respect and adapt to the person's shape. Thus, it is very important to carefully observe the particularities of the figure; to know how to take precise measurements; and understand how to apply them in such a way that the basic pattern will conform to the shape of the body. The approach is precise and meticulous, so this book has very detailed explanations for the use and application of every line of the draft. It covers every element necessary for creating a made-to-measure pattern in order to achieve an exact imprint, in two-dimensional form, of the figure's shape.

VIRTUAL LINES

A bespoke pattern is an exact imprint of the body. Based on measurements taken of the figure, the pattern creates a two-dimensional representation. The shape and size of the body are reproduced by a drawing on a piece of paper, which we call a "flat pattern." To create this drawing, we use virtual lines that we apply to the figure, which serve as reference points for transferring the measurements of length and width. Each of these lines plays a very precise role and each one is essential. Leaving out even one line can distort the entire construction of the pattern.

Vertical lines (sagittal lines). The length measurements: the length of the back, front, or the bust, for example. These lines are also necessary for correctly positioning the perpendicular horizontal lines, such as the upper chest line, armhole line, or full hip line. They are also used to ensure the exact placement of the darts.

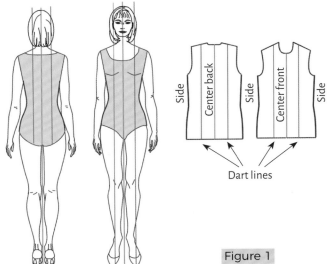

Figure 1

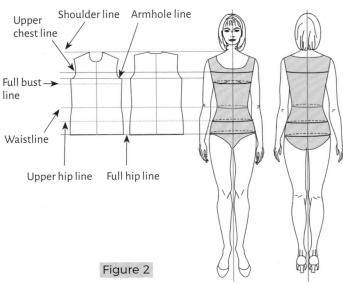

Figure 2

Horizontal lines (transverse lines). These are the lines where we apply the contour measurements (such as the full bust or full hip circumference) and width measurements (width of the back, front upper-chest width, or bust point to bust point, for example). It is very important to draw these lines strictly perpendicular to the vertical lines (use a tailor's square or L-square to ensure this)—otherwise the garment may not drape correctly.

MAIN PATTERN LINES

The pattern outline is made up of various kinds of lines that differ in importance depending on how they are used: the indication and application of the measurements, and/or the transformation of the basic pattern into a finished pattern. In order for the pattern to be well adapted to the shape of the body, it is absolutely essential that all of the virtual lines and their proportions (which are specific to each person) be indicated on the drawing. The correspondence between the virtual lines on the figure and the lines drawn on the paper must be exact. In order to make this happen, we need to rely on the classification of the different roles given to each type of line, which are presented below.

REFERENCE LINES

These lines are absolutely indispensable. They constitute the foundation on which the pattern is built. They serve as reference points for applying all of the measurements of the body. The two vertical reference lines are the center back line and the center front line. They divide the body in two: the right side and the left side. It is based on these two lines that we can establish the measurements of the widths and contours of the body.

The third reference line, the waistline, is horizontal. It divides the body into the upper part (the bodice) and the lower part (the legs). Depending on what is needed, we can take measurements *to* the waist (such as for the length of the back of a vest) or *from* the waist (such as for the length of a skirt or a pair of pants). In the same way, these measurements are applied to the pattern outline.

11

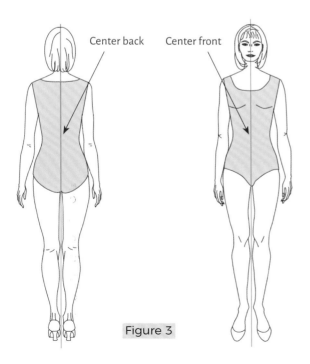

Center back   Center front

Figure 3

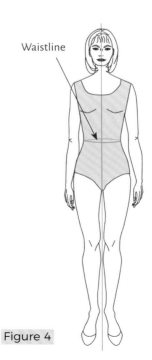

Waistline

Figure 4

CONSTRUCTION LINES

These lines can be horizontal or vertical depending on the application of the various measurements that have been taken (Figure 5): contour lines (full hip line for the circumference of the hip, for example); height lines (such as the height of the full bust); length lines (for instance of the back); or width lines (such as the front upper-chest width). The placement of these construction lines will depend on the figure's proportions, shape, and outline.

AUXILIARY LINES

These are lines that you can draw depending on your needs. For instance, the upper hip line will need to be drawn if the skirt pattern has a yoke or pockets; the full bust line will need to be drawn if the bodice pattern uses darts (Figure 6). If the pattern does not include any of these details, there is no need to draw those lines—it overloads the pattern and can make it hard to read.

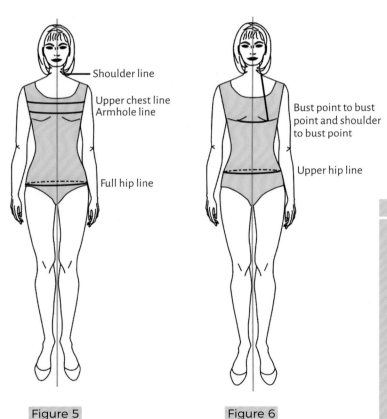

Shoulder line

Upper chest line
Armhole line

Full hip line

Bust point to bust point and shoulder to bust point

Upper hip line

Figure 5

Figure 6

A Good Thing to Know

To make progress in creating basic patterns, it is essential to have a good understanding of the usefulness and purpose of construction lines. This is a fundamental step. The rest of the construction work of the garment depends on this.

FROM DRAFT PATTERN TO FINISHED PATTERN

The drawing of a pattern includes all the vertical and horizontal lines that are indicated virtually on the body (see Figures 5 and 6, opposite).

Before getting to the pattern that will be used to cut the various pieces of fabric to create the desired final piece, there are several stages of construction to follow. At each of them, different lines are added. These lines are identified by how they are used: there are lines that are used for the basic pattern, lines used for the fitting pattern (basic corrections and checks), the lines that apply the modifications, and the lines of the cutting pattern.

You don't need to copy over the pattern at every stage of construction. In general, all the lines that serve to gradually transform the flat pattern into a finished pattern (or cutting pattern) are applied to the same outline.

For the final draft to be clear and legible, and for every step to be well indicated and easily identifiable, the lines of each step need to be distinguished from each other, for example by using a color code such as the one used in this book.

- Reference lines: —————— in red
- Basic construction lines: —————— in black
- Enlargement lines: —————— in green
- Manipulation lines: —————— in blue

FLAT PATTERN

This draft is the two-dimensional representation of the imprint of the body: it respects the body's shape and pro-portions, as well as the distribution of darts according to measurements. It is never used for cutting the fabric, nor even for applying corrections. In order to be able to use this draft, the basic enlargements have to be added to the contour measurements and to certain height measure-ments, as can be seen on Figure 8 on the next page.

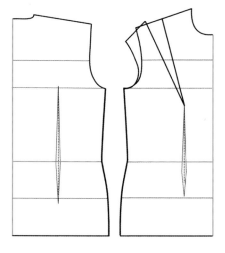

Figure 7

FITTING PATTERN

The template that is created from the measurements must then be checked and, often, corrected. Even if the measurements have been taken very precisely, they will not, for example, account for the rounding of the back or the curve of the hip.

In order to be able to attach the bodice and correct how it drapes, there is a minimum amount of enlargement that must be added (in green, Figure 8). This basic enlargement includes both the width of the fabric and the assembly seam allowances (see page 67). It is based on this fitting pattern, after the corrections have been added, that we obtain the basic finished pattern, which is the subject of this book.

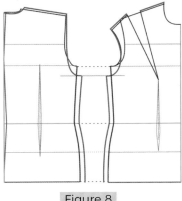

Figure 8

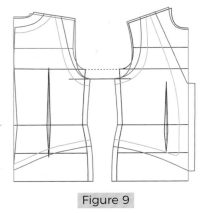

Figure 9

MODIFIED PATTERN

This step consists of applying manipulations to the pattern that has already been adjusted and corrected in the preceding step to obtain a drawing of the desired model.

We use different colors to identify at a glance the lines of the flat pattern (in black); the enlargements (in green); and the manipulations (in blue). On the same drawing, we will use another color (here we use orange) to indicate such elements as facings and accessories. Then, trace the different parts of the pattern by following the line in the appropriate color (a necessary step before getting to the finished pattern).

FINISHED PATTERN

This is the final pattern for the garment, which includes not only all the modifications made to the basic pattern but also the seam allowances, the reference notches and assembly notches, the indications about straight-grain and cross-grain, any labels, etc. (see Figure 109, page 68).

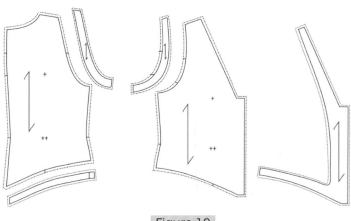

Figure 10

IMPORTANT FEATURES OF THE PATTERN

Before starting to draw the pattern, there are certain elements that need to be noted to avoid possible errors during construction.

CONSTRUCTION OF THE BACK AND THE FRONT

All basic patterns, whether they are bodices, skirts, or pants, are drawn with a half-front and a half-back (Figure 11). Excepting asymmetrical clothing, the section that has been drawn as a half will be cut on the fold of the fabric to create the exact same shape on either side of the center back line and/or the center front line, creating an entire back or front pattern.

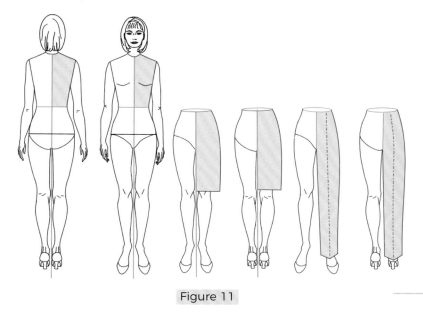

Figure 11

SLEEVE CONSTRUCTION

The exception to the rule stated above is the draft of the sleeve. The basic sleeve is constructed based on the shape and measurements of the bodice's armhole (see page 93). For the sleeve, the drawing will represent both the back part and the front part, which will be divided by a mark (a red line in Figure 12) that must correspond to the bodice's shoulder line.

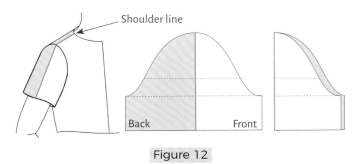

Shoulder line

Back   Front

Figure 12

Unlike the other elements (bodice, skirt, and pants), the sleeve has no center line, because the width of the back of the sleeve is always different from the width of the front of the sleeve. This difference also depends on the slope of the shoulder, which varies depending on body shape. The vertical line (in red, Figure 12) drawn along the length of the sleeve is a reference point to which various measurements—how high the sleeve cap is, how wide the back and front are—are applied for defining how the sleeve drapes (see page 115, fitting).

POSITIONING THE SIDE LINE

To determine the width of the half-back and half-front, and in order to place the side line on the pattern draft, we divide the circumference of the full bust by four. But if we assume those quadrants are of equal dimensions, the side line will end up too far forward (Figure 13).

In Figure 13, the placement of the side line throws off the armhole curvature (the back and front parts are no longer in proportion), making the sleeve construction impossible. It is essential to restore the correct positioning of the side line by moving it toward the back. To get a correctly positioned side line, move it one centimeter toward the back of the garment (Figure 14).

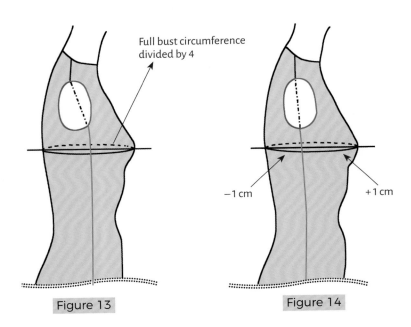

Full bust circumference divided by 4

−1 cm   +1 cm

Figure 13   Figure 14

FLATTENING

Flattening refers to the flat lines at the ends of curvatures. This allows us to avoid sharp points, beaks, or hollows during assembly, or after unfolding the fabric cut on the fold. It is very important to respect the flat line of the center back, the center front, and especially those of the armhole (green circles in Figure 15).

Figure 16 shows what you should definitely not do: here there are no flat line segments—only curves. It will be impossible to connect the sleeve with the armhole.

On the outline of the pattern, flat lines also need to be applied to various other areas, like bust points, darts, the waist, etc. (see Figure 117, page 75).

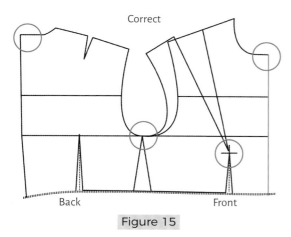

Correct

Back   Front

Figure 15

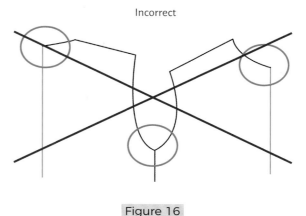

Incorrect

Figure 16

NOTCHES

Notches play an essential role in the assembly of the garment. They must be positioned on the finished pattern and then copied over to the fabric during cutting. On the pattern, a notch is indicated by a small mark placed along the line of the drawing. On the fabric it is indicated by a short cutout along the edge of about 2 to 3 millimeters. There are two kinds of notches:

- **Assembly notches** are used to match two elements of a piece of clothing together, for instance at the waist line, the full bust line, or the full hip line. There are no rules for how to position them. In principle, they should be present on all construction lines, but in practice, they are put wherever they are needed to make assembly as easy and accurate as possible.

- **Reference notches** are used to identify pieces of the pattern. Putting a notch at the top of a sleeve, for example, makes it possible to easily differentiate between the back and the front. Or, in the example of a paneled skirt made up of several elements of similar shape, the reference notches will identify each element individually so you'll avoid mixing them up.

17

Note

Even if the drawing of the pattern is correct, if the assembly is carried out without matching the notches accurately, the garment could be distorted, throwing off the drape line.

TAKING MEASUREMENTS

For the draft of your customized pattern to be as faithful as possible to the template and to the figure, the measurements must be taken very precisely. Do not hesitate to ask for help from a third person. Any mistakes that you make while taking the measurements can be corrected later, during the fitting, but this is time-consuming and fastidious work that often requires starting over several times. What that entails is tracing the pattern again according to the measurements, cutting the fabric to the pattern, trying it on, applying the corrections to the fabric, transferring them to the pattern; and then, once again, cutting the fabric, and then trying the pattern again to verify it. And if it still isn't right (for instance, if the bodice does not drape correctly), the entire process will start all over again from the beginning. In other words, you save time and gain precision by taking good and careful measurements to begin with.

Some tailors add seam allowances at the time the measurements are taken. But, while there are undeniable merits to this method, it does have to be noted that a pattern constructed in this way can only be used once and for one single design. The necessary allowances will vary according to the type and style of clothing (coat, casual clothing, suit, wide tunic, etc.), the quality of the fabric, and the preferences of the individual (for a more or less close fit).

TAKING MEASUREMENTS FOR THE BODICE

BACK MEASUREMENTS

Back Length

This measurement, which might seem like a very simple one, requires special attention because of how important it is in the construction of the pattern.

Very many techniques recommend starting from the first cervical vertebra at the center of the back, and proceeding from there to the waist. This method is very easy because the knob of the cervical vertebra is a precise and easily identifiable reference point, but this method does not take into account the rounding of the back at the level of the shoulder blades. But that rounding is different for every body and thus has to be included in the measurements. In measuring the length of the back, use the base of the neck along the shoulder line, measuring from there to the waist (Figure 17).

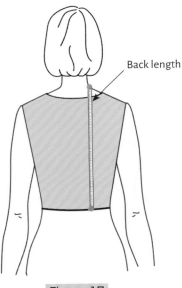

Back length

Figure 17

Shoulder Length or Back Width

The choice between these two measurements depends on the shape of the body. The length of the shoulder is relevant for slim, well-proportioned people. But it can turn out to be a complicated thing for bodies with short, thick necks. Also, if the back is very rounded, that rounding will not be taken into account.

- Shoulder length: Distance from the neck to the bony point of the end of the shoulder (acromion) (Figure 18, left)
- Back width: Distance between the bony points of the ends of the two shoulders (Figure 18, right)

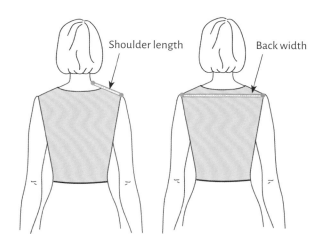

Shoulder length

Back width

Figure 18

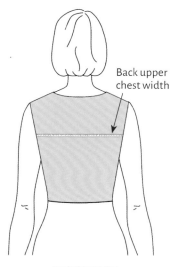

Back upper chest width

Figure 19

Width of the Back Upper Chest

To determine the width of the back upper chest, we measure the distance from one arm to the other at the point where the arms connect to the body. This measurement allows us to determine where the armhole curve starts and the side line. It is a very important measurement because it indicates how wide the sleeve cap should be, thereby contributing to the correct drape of the sleeve. If this measurement is not taken correctly, the sleeve cap can gape (because it is too wide) or interfere with the movements of the arm (because it is too narrow).

FRONT MEASUREMENTS

Front Length

The length of the front is measured from the base of the neck along the shoulder line to the waist, passing through the bust point (Figure 20). It is essential for this measurement to pass through the bust point (it should not pass between the two breasts) so that the size of the bust is taken into account.

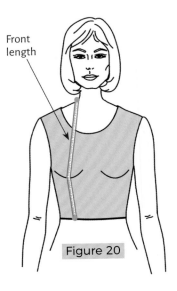

Front length

Figure 20

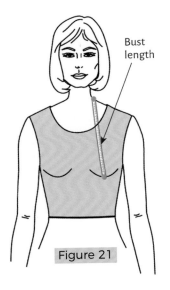

Bust length

Figure 21

Bust Length

The length of the bust is measured from the base of the neck at the shoulder line to the bust point.

This measurement allows you to determine the height of the waist dart (see page 54) or the shape and placement of the curve of the bust in the case of a front shoulder cutout or princess seam, for example. When you are drawing the pattern, you have to take into account the flat lines of the bust, which allow you to give the garment a lovely shape (Figure 15, page 17).

Front Upper Chest Width

For this measurement, we proceed as in the back: by measuring the distance from one arm to the other at the point where the arms join the body. It is interesting to note that the front upper chest width is always smaller than the back upper chest width. If both your measurements end up the same, you have made a mistake and will need to remeasure. As with the back, this measurement is very important for the construction of the sleeve. If the measurement is too wide, the sleeve cap will gape; if it is too narrow, there will not be enough room for the arms to move.

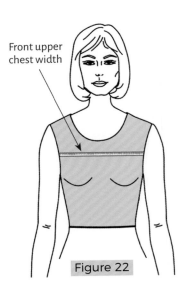

Front upper chest width

Figure 22

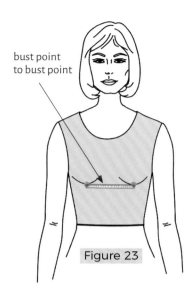

bust point
to bust point

Figure 23

Bust Point to Bust Point

For the bust-point-to-bust-point length, measure the distance between the bust points (the outermost points of the breasts). This measurement must be taken very carefully because the placement of the cutting lines and the darts depend on it (Figure 38, page 26).

The Use of Extra Measurements

Using the bust point as a reference allows us to take two measurements that will help us when we are reviewing the basic pattern and correcting the depth of the neckline and the slope of the shoulder (see page 51). These measurements do not contribute to the construction of the pattern and do not change the steps involved in drafting it.

Neckline Depth

Because it is hard to accurately measure the circumference of the neck (Figure 26, page 22), we can take a measurement from the center front, at the level of the two clavicle bones, to the bust point, to help determine the depth of the neckline (Figure 24).

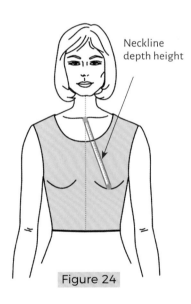

Neckline
depth height

Figure 24

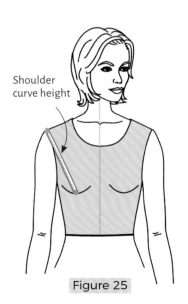

Shoulder
curve height

Figure 25

Shoulder Curve Height

This measurement is taken from the bust point to the bony point at the edge of the shoulder (acromion) (Figure 25). Using the two measurements of bust length (Figure 27, opposite) and shoulder curve height, we can obtain the shoulder slope particular to the person's shape.

MEASURING CONTOURS

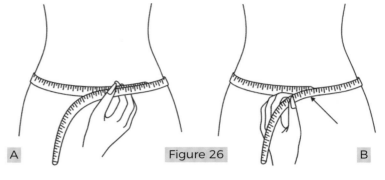

It isn't easy to measure contours, because keeping the tape measure perfectly horizontal all around the person's body is not straightforward. To make it easier, people tend to put their fingers between the tape measure and the skin (Figure 26A). But measurements taken in this way will thus be widened in an undesirable way because the difference that the fingers make will not be identical along all the contours (bust, waist, hips, etc.) of the body.

Figure 26

The way to measure contours correctly is illustrated in Figure 26B. Any necessary enlargements will be added later, either from the basic pattern or from the specific model being made, because the size of the required enlargement will change depending on the type of clothing (coat, jacket, shirt) and the style.

Neck Circumference

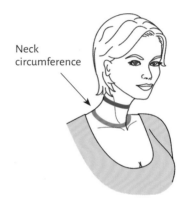

Neck circumference

Figure 27

Like most contour measurements, this measurement is not easy to make. The contour measurement taken at the middle of the neck (in green, Figure 27) theoretically corresponds to the size of the neck circumference. But since the neckline is made up of two unequal parts, the back and the front, this measurement must be taken at the base of the neck (in red, Figure 27) to allow for its width and the varying depths (front and back) in the construction of the basic pattern.

Body Circumference at Upper Chest Height

This measurement is taken by placing the tape measure all around the body along the upper chest, with the arms slightly apart and relaxed along the length of the body.

This measurement will be used when constructing the sleeve cap, to check its width and, if necessary, to correct it. This measurement is also used in the construction of cloaks cut on the grain and capes.

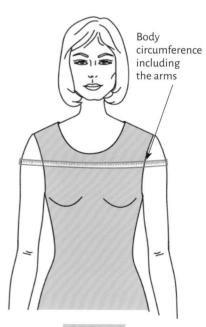

Body circumference including the arms

Figure 28

Full Bust Circumference

In order to take this measurement correctly, make sure that the tape measure is perfectly horizontal in the back, and that in the front it passes through the fullest part of the bust (at the bust points). In the construction of the basic pattern, this measurement is used to determine the width of the upper part of the bodice, so it is important that it be made very precisely.

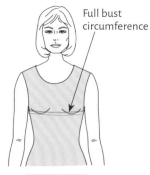

Figure 29

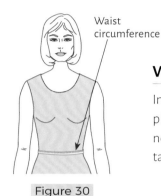

Figure 30

Waist Circumference

In order to take this measurement correctly, a ribbon or string must first be placed around the waist. Check that it is placed perfectly horizontally (it should not ride up or down in the back or the front, for instance because of a belly). Then take the measurement by placing the tape measure along the ribbon (Figure 30).

Full Hip Circumference

As with the waist, you can use a ribbon to make sure that you are taking this measurement correctly. Place the ribbon at full hip height (determined by establishing the hip length in the following step), making sure that this height is parallel to the line of the waist all around the body. Thus, the ribbon will be positioned perfectly horizontally. Measure the full hip circumference by following the ribbon. This measurement is important because it will determine the width of the lower part of the bodice on the basic pattern.

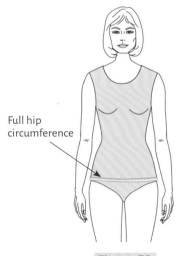

Figure 31

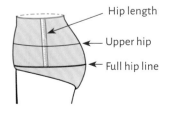

Figure 32

Full Hip Length

The full hip length corresponds to the vertical distance between the waist line and the horizontal line at the widest part of the hips. This measurement serves as a reference point to establish the full hip line in making the pattern.

Upper Hip Length

The upper hip line is positioned halfway between the waist and the full hip line. This line, which is not used for construction (Figure 6, page 12), is only drawn on the pattern when necessary—either to position the pockets or if there is a yoke or cut lines (see page 186).

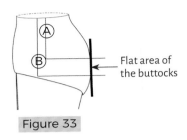

Figure 33

A Good Thing to Know

Most of the time, it is not immediately obvious how to correctly determine hip length, since it depends on the shape and size of the buttocks, and the length of the flat area at the back of the buttocks can range anywhere from 5 to 8 cm. Thus, hip length can be fixed anywhere along the line of this flat area (Figure 33). Thus, the different measurements of hip length (see A and B) affect the upper hip line, since that is always positioned halfway between the waistline and the full hip line. According to the French clothing federation (FDA), which is responsible for standard measurement charts, the vertical length from the waist to the hip varies from 17 to 23 cm for all heights. To avoid incorrect placement of lines, the construction of basic patterns takes this information into account and positions the hip length at a medium measurement of 20 cm. The length of the upper hip line is 10 cm. Most pattern makers and their methods and techniques of constructing basic patterns use this average measurement.

ARM MEASUREMENTS

This measurement must be taken with the arm bent, because the difference between the measurement of an extended arm and a bent arm, depending on the person's height and shape, can be between 2 and 3 cm. If we take this measurement on an extended arm, the resulting sleeve may be uncomfortable, hampering the movements of the arm (especially for patterns with cuffed sleeves).

Shoulder-to-Elbow Arm Length

This distance is measured from the shoulder bone (acromion) to the elbow bone on a bent arm. This measurement allows us to make a basic sleeve into a suit-jacket sleeve or a cuffed sleeve, for example, where the position of the dart plays an important role.

For a short sleeve, on the other hand, we only measure the distance to the inside of the bend to the forearm (green line, Figure 34), which will allow for greater comfort in arm movements.

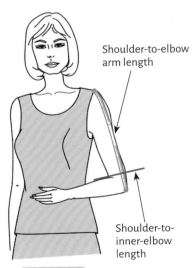

Shoulder-to-elbow arm length

Shoulder-to-inner-elbow length

Figure 34

Arm Length

This is measured on a bent arm, from the shoulder bone (acromion) to the wrist bone, taking care to take the elbow into account.

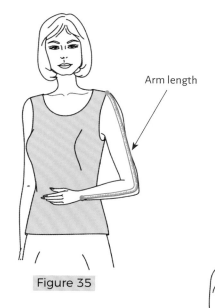

Arm length

Figure 35

Arm Circumference

The arm circumference is measured at the widest point of the arm. This measurement makes sure that the sleeve width is accurate. In the method presented here, the width of the sleeve depends on how much the garment is enlarged and the length of the armhole. At the same time, in a custom construction, it is important to take into account the measurement of the arm circumference, which can vary greatly depending on a person's shape.

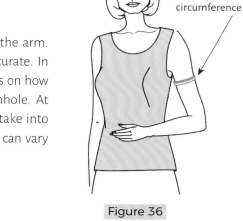

Arm circumference

Figure 36

Wrist Circumference

For this measurement, we place a tape measure around the wrist at the level of the wrist bone (at the widest part).

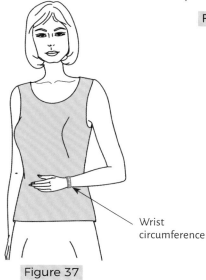

Wrist circumference

Figure 37

TAKING MEASUREMENTS FOR THE SKIRT

The main measurements used to construct a basic skirt pattern are seen in Figure 38.

- The bust-point-to-bust-point measurement (Figure 23, page 21)—in other words, the distance between the bust points—is used for placing the front darts. On the pattern draft, the vertical lines that start at the bust point and run perpendicular to the bust line correspond to the axis of the skirt's waist darts (as is also true for the bodice's waist darts);
- the waist circumference (Figure 30, page 23);
- the full hip circumference (Figure 31, page 23);
- the skirt length (Figure 39).

In general, the measurement of the **skirt length** is taken along the line of the side from the waist down to the desired length. However, in custom construction, this must be adapted to the person's shape. If the person has a large belly or prominent buttocks, for example, further measurements will be required: in this case, the length of the skirt in the center of the back and the center of the front. These measurements will be used to accurately draw the curvature of the waistline according to the shaping of the darts.

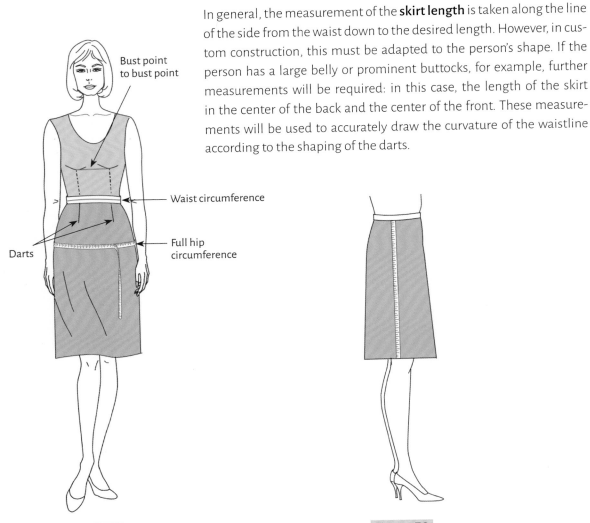

Bust point
to bust point

Waist circumference

Full hip
circumference

Darts

Figure 38

Figure 39

TAKING MEASUREMENTS FOR PANTS

To create a basic pattern for trousers, you'll be measuring the parts of the body below the waist. Some of these measurements are used for the creation of the pants pattern, while others are used to double-check the drawing, such as the thigh circumference, calf circumference, or the crotch length.

CONTOUR MEASUREMENTS

① **Waist circumference:** This measurement is taken the same way as for the bodice or the skirt (see Figure 30, page 23).

② **Full hip circumference:** This measurement is taken the same way as for the bodice or the skirt (see Figure 32, page 23).

③ **Thigh circumference:** To take this measurement, place the tape measure at the widest part of the thigh. This measurement allows you to make sure that the width of the leg below the crotch line (see Figure 40), obtained according to the basic pattern, is adapted to the person's shape. This becomes particularly necessary when creating customized patterns if the body has very developed upper thighs or lower buttocks.

④ **Calf circumference:** This measurement is taken at the widest point of the calf, between the knee and the ankle depending on the person's shape.

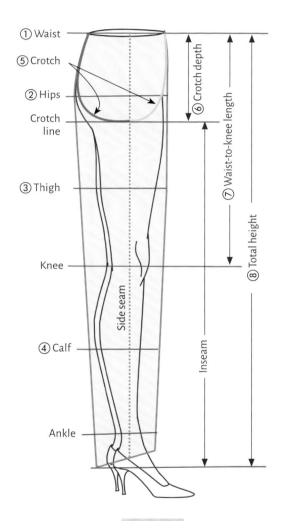

Figure 40

27

PANTS BOTTOM WIDTH

To ensure that the bottom of the pants is wide enough and allows for the garment to be put on easily, one more measurement is necessary: the measurement of the foot circumference (Figure 41). This measurement is taken with the foot extended (in the same position as one would use for putting on a pair of pants) from the tip of the heel to the instep.

Figure 41

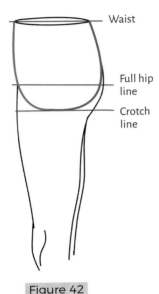

— Waist

— Full hip line

— Crotch line

Figure 42

HEIGHT MEASUREMENTS

⑤ **Crotch length**: The way this measurement is traditionally taken— from the center back of the waist to the center front of the waist, passing between the legs (Figure 42, green and blue lines)—this measurement is imperfect, because it does not take into account the size of the buttocks, given that the tape measure passes through the middle of the buttocks cleft. We will not use it in the rest of this book except to check the crotch pattern created according to our method (see chapter 5, "Pants," p. 137).

⑥ **Crotch depth**: This measurement, difficult to make, is the most important one in the creation of the pants pattern, because the crotch pattern depends on the precision of this measurement. It varies according to the height and shape of the person's body. Of the several existing techniques, the simplest and most reliable consists of sitting the person on a very straight support (such as a stool) and then, using a ruler placed perpendicularly, to mark the distance from the waist to the support.

Figure 43

⑦ **Waist-to-knee length**: As for the skirt length, this measurement is taken along the side line (see Figure 29, page 26). For greater precision, take the measurement at the rounded part of the knee, with the leg lightly bent. When constructing based on standard measurements, knee height is between 55 and 60 cm. Barring exceptional cases, these measurements hold for all different heights.

⑧ **Total height**: Even though this measurement might seem very easy to make, it still must not be neglected. Very often, the total length of the pants depends on the cut of the base of the pants, either straight across (Figures 45A and C) or on the bias (Figure 45B and D). The length of the pants also changes depending on the height of the heels. Thus, it is preferable to take heel height into account when measuring total height.

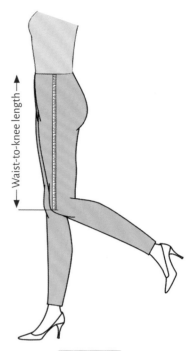

Figure 44

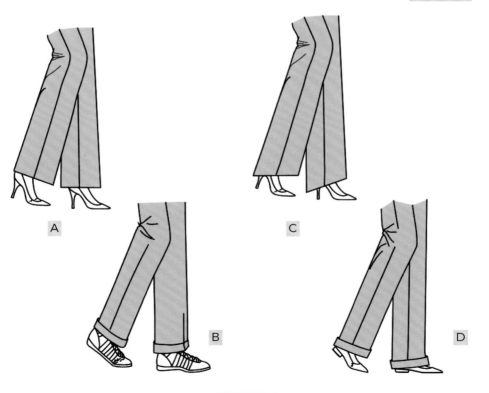

A

C

B

D

Figure 45

THE BODICE

It is not that hard to create a basic pattern, even using personalized measurements, if we take the time to understand why we must draw each of the lines. What they are used for? What is the role they play in construction, their impact on how the garment drapes, or the visual effect that they produce on the finished piece?

In this chapter, you will find step-by-step instructions for drawing a pattern, with in-depth explanations for each step. The successful creation of a pattern depends not only on scrupulously following the directions given here, but also on a solid understanding of the reasons for following those directions.

DRAFTING THE PATTERN
TO MEASURE

The first step in drafting the basic flat pattern consists of representing the body in two dimensions by transcribing it into a template.

Drafting the pattern always starts with the drawing of the back. This is the most reliable method because the back is much less affected by the body's shapes, unlike the front, whose length will have to take into account the size of the bust, which may be smaller or larger.

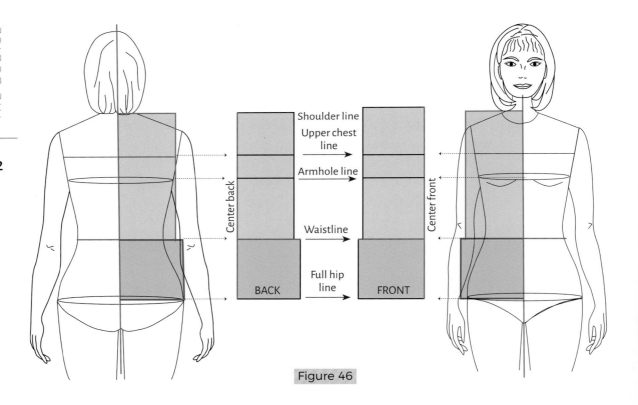

Figure 46

You can see here how the virtual lines of the body and the construction lines of the paper pattern draft correspond to each other.

BACK TEMPLATE

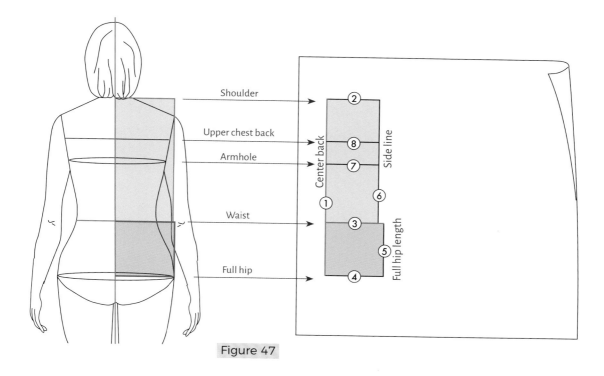

Figure 47

① The first line of the draft is the reference line of the center back. Draw it in red at about 5 cm from the edge of the paper and make it somewhere between 60 and 70 cm long. This length is made up of two measurements added together: the length of the back (Figure 17, page 18) and the full hip length (Figure 32, page 23). The exact measurement will be determined later.

② Then draw (in black) a horizontal line about 7 to 10 cm from the top of the paper: this is the shoulder line.

③ Starting from the shoulder line, follow the center-back line down the distance of the measurement of the length of the back, and at that point, make a line perpendicular to the center back: this is the waistline. This, too, is a reference line, so it also must be drawn in red.

④ Starting from the waistline, follow the center-back line down again, this time for the measurement of the full hip length. At that point, draw another perpendicular line: this is the full hip line (this is in black, like all the lines drawn for points 5 to 8 of the back construction).

Note

The side line for the bodice depends on two measurements: the bust circumference and the full hip circumference. To draw this line, we must start at the shoulder line and go down to the waist (using the measurement of the bust circumference), and then go from the waist to the full hip line (using the measurement of the full hip circumference).

⑤ In order to draw the part of the side line that corresponds to the full hip length, divide the measurement of the full hip circumference by 4, then subtract 1 cm. Starting at the point where the full hip line intersects with the center-back line, follow the full hip line out the distance of that measurement. At that point, draw a line perpendicular to the full hip line up to the waistline.

⑥ In order to draw the part of the side line that corresponds to the distance from waist to shoulder, divide the measurement of the bust circumference by 4 and then subtract 1 cm. Starting at the point where the shoulder line intersects with the center-back line, follow the shoulder line out the distance of that measurement. At that point, draw a line perpendicular to the shoulder line down to the waistline.

⑦ For the armhole line, draw a horizontal line halfway between the shoulder line and the waistline (using the distance of the shoulder length divided by 2), connecting the center-back line to the side line.

⑧ To draw the upper chest line, take 1/3 of the distance from the shoulder line to the armhole line. Beginning at the point where the armhole line intersects with the center-back line, follow the center-back line up that distance from the armhole line and at that point, draw a horizontal line over to the side line.

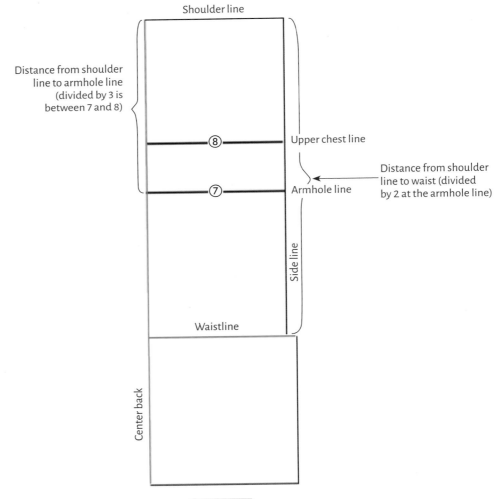

Figure 48

FRONT TEMPLATE

After drawing the template for the half-back, we will now draw the template for the half-front. In a mirrored construction (see Figure 49), transfer all the horizontal lines from the half-back template (full hips, arm-hole, and upper chest in black; waist in red) to the half-front template; the exception is the shoulder line, which will be drawn later (see step 10 below).

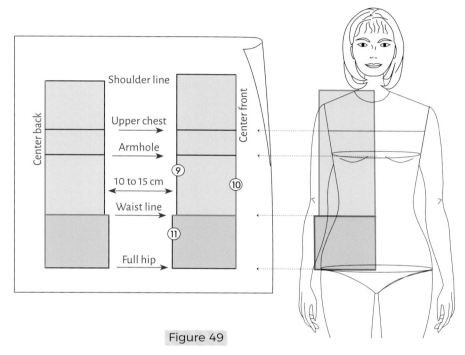

Figure 49

⑨ Draw a parallel line from the shoulder line (defined below in step 10) to the waistline, about 10 to 15 cm away from the side line of the back template.

⑩ Measure the width of the front by dividing the bust circumference by 4, then adding 1 cm.
Now draw a vertical line, parallel to the side line and separated from the side line by the measurement obtained above: this is the center-front line. This is a reference line, thus it must be drawn in red.
Along this line, starting from the horizontal waist line, measure up by the amount of the front length (see Figure 20, page 20).
Starting at the point thus arrived at, draw a horizontal line over to the front side line: this is the shoulder line.

⑪ In order to determine the width of the lower part of the bodice (green rectangle, Figure 49), divide the full hip circumference by 4, then add 1 cm (see the explanations in Figures 13 and 14, page 16). Take this measurement and draw it out along the waistline, starting from the point where the waistline intersects with the center-front line. At the end point of that measurement, draw a line downward, perpendicular to the waistline, to meet the full hip line.

UPPER HIP LINE

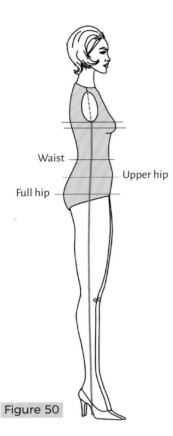

Figure 50

Using the upper hip line in drafting the basic pattern requires some explanation, because it is a controversial subject among professionals. It is not the placement of the line that is problematic, but rather, taking the measurement of the circumference of the upper hip on the body, and then integrating it into the draft as a construction line.

In the pattern construction method presented in this book, the upper hip line is not considered a construction line, but an auxiliary line—to help in positioning cutouts, yokes, pockets, etc. (Figure 51). The measurement of the circumference of the body at the level of the upper hips is not exact, because even though it includes the size of the stomach, it does not take the size of the buttocks into account (Figure 50), so it cannot be used to establish the width of the back and the front of the pattern. As a result, it is problematic in most cases to draw the side line while taking the circumferences of the waist, the upper hips, and the full hips into account all at the same time.

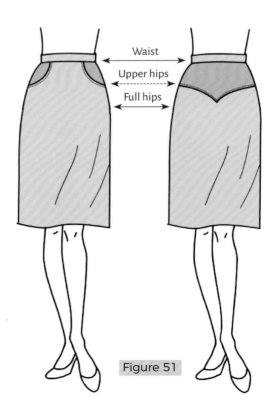

Figure 51

Let's look at drafting patterns for rounded body shapes (with well-developed bellies and/or buttocks), whose proportions are sometimes very different from those on standard patterns. In order to make sure the size of the belly is accounted for, you will have to take a partial measurement (starting from the side line) at the level of the upper hips (green line, Figure 52). To complete the measurement of this part of the body, you will have to measure the size of the buttocks at the level of the full hips, starting from the side line (blue line, Figure 52).

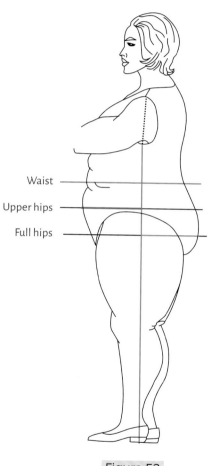

Figure 52

CHECKING YOUR MEASUREMENTS

We have now drafted the templates for the half-back and the half-front (width and length) including the most important construction lines.

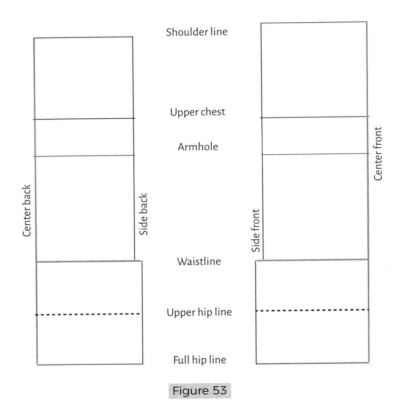

Figure 53

The next task is to determine the shapes of the neckline and armhole. Before going on to this step, take the time to check that you have transferred the measurements and placed the construction lines (both vertical and horizontal) correctly. This first step of the construction is the most important: if you've made a mistake here, the whole pattern will be inaccurate. The two frames of the figure outline shown in Figure 53 include the upper hip line: this line, placed halfway between the waist and the full hip line, is an auxiliary line (see page 12, "Auxiliary lines").

NECKLINE

To determine the outline and shape of the neckline, we refer to the measurement of the neck circumference. This drawing is in two parts: The back neckline, on the pattern of the center back, and the front neckline, calculated based on the back neckline (in green, Figure 54). These lines are drawn on the pattern of the center front-back and on the front (in blue, Figure 54).

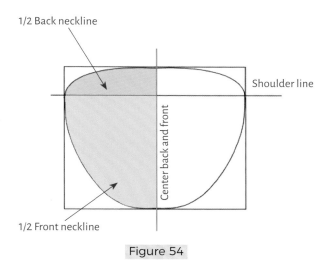

1/2 Back neckline

Shoulder line

Center back and front

1/2 Front neckline

Figure 54

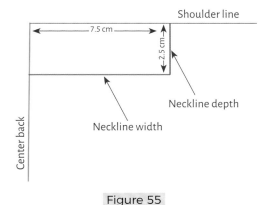

Shoulder line

7.5 cm

2.5 cm

Neckline depth

Neckline width

Center back

Figure 55

BACK NECKLINE

The two measurements that are essential for defining the shape of the neckline are the width of the neckline (green line, Figure 55) and the depth of the neckline (blue line, Figure 55).

Neckline Width

To obtain the measurement of the neckline width, measure the circumference of the neck (Figure 27, page 22), divide that by 6, and add 1 cm. *For example, if the neck circumference is 38 cm, then 38 divided by 6 is 6.33, and if you add 1 to that you get 7.33 (this measurement can be rounded up—in this case to 7.5 cm).*

Now take this neckline width measurement and transfer it to the shoulder line, starting at the center back line (red line, Figure 55). Then, at the endpoint of the neckline width measurement, draw a short vertical line (blue line, Figure 55), to which you will transfer the neckline depth measurement after you have calculated it (see following step).

39

Neckline Depth

To measure the neckline depth, measure the neck circumference, then divide it by 16. *For example, if the neck circumference is 38 cm, then 38 divided by 16 is 2.38 cm (this measurement can be rounded up—in this case to 2.5 cm).* Transfer this measurement onto the vertical line (blue line, Figure 55).

As a general rule, for sizes 4 through 16, this measurement is somewhere between 2 and 3 cm. However, for the most accurate possible pattern draft, it is best to work with an exact measurement—it's worth your while to make the calculation described above.

FRONT NECKLINE

Along the shoulder line, starting from the center front, transfer the measurement of the back neckline width (in the previous example, 7.5 cm). At that point, draw a line perpendicular to the shoulder line (blue line, Figure 56).

To get the measurement of the neckline depth in the front, add 2 cm to the neckline width. *For example, if the neckline width is 7.5 cm, add 2 to get 9.5 cm.*

Transfer this measurement to the vertical line (in blue). At that point, draw a perpendicular that will go back to join the center front line (green line, Figure 56).

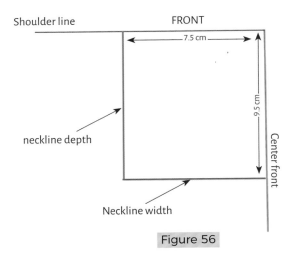

Figure 56

Note

At this stage of the construction, the neck outline is only indicated by straight lines. The neckline curve will be drawn when checking the pattern (pages 63–64).

SHOULDER SLOPE AND LENGTH

BACK SHOULDER

In the first chapter, you saw that it is better, in certain cases, to measure the length from the neck to the shoulder rather than the width of the back between the two shoulder points (Figure 18, page 19). Now, you will see in detail how to use both these measurements to determine the slope of the shoulder on the back pattern.

Using the Shoulder Length Measurement

At the end of the neckline width, along the shoulder line, draw a straight line forming an 18-degree angle with the shoulder line (blue line). Along this line, transfer the measurement of the shoulder length, then indicate its endpoint with a vertical line (dotted green line, Figure 57).

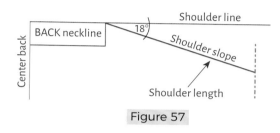

Figure 57

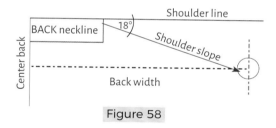

Figure 58

Using the Back Width Measurement

Transfer the measurement of the back width (dotted black line, Figure 58), starting from the center back (red line). Indicate its endpoint with a vertical line (dotted green line). At the end of the neckline width, draw a straight line forming an 18-degree angle with the shoulder line (blue line) to the intersection point between these two dotted lines (circle).

FRONT SHOULDER

At the end of the neckline width, at the shoulder line, draw a straight line making a 26-degree angle with the shoulder line (blue line). Then, along this line, transfer the measurement of the back shoulder length. Indicate the endpoint of this measurement with a vertical line (green dotted line, Figure 59).

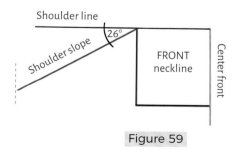

Figure 59

BACK AND FRONT ARMHOLE

For this drawing, it is crucial that you follow the order of the steps indicated here (Figure 60). The shape of the armhole cannot be established unless the 4 points for the back and the 4 points for the front (in blue) are positioned correctly.

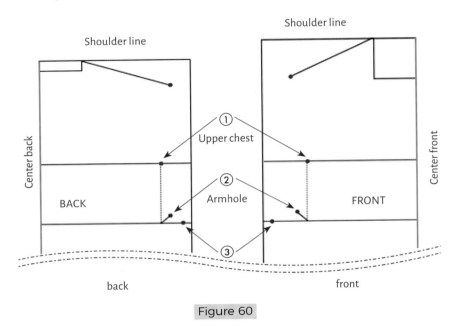

Figure 60

① On the upper chest line, starting from the center back line, measure half of the width of the back upper chest (blue dots; see also Figure 19, page 19). Then, at that width, draw a perpendicular line (dotted black line) to the armhole line. In the same way, measure half the width of the front upper chest along the front upper chest line and draw the perpendicular line there down to the armhole line as well.

(see also Figure 19, page 19)

Note

The measurements along the bisecting lines are reference points, but the drawing of the armhole curves may end up changing them. These numbers depend on the person's shape, and can vary depending on which measurement is used: the width of the front and back upper chest, for example, or the measurement of the bust circumference.

② Along a line bisecting the angle between the perpendicular line you just drew and the armhole line (a line rising at 45 degrees), measure 1.5 cm on the back and 2.5 cm on the front (blue dots).

③ It is extremely important to indicate the flat areas along the armhole line: starting from the side line, measure 1 cm and make a mark along the armhole line (blue dots; see also page 16). These flat area markings can be corrected, if necessary, during the fitting.

USING A FRENCH CURVE RULER

To draw the armhole, you must join all 8 points (in blue, Figure 60, page 42) using a French curve ruler. You can find all sorts of curved tools on the market that will help you to draw rounded lines—the French curve ruler shown on these pages, which has several different choices of curves, can be very easily adapted to a variety of patterns.

Positioning the French Curve

Even if you have very carefully applied the measurements of the shoulder length, upper chest, and full bust circumference to the pattern, the shape of the armhole will not be right if you use the French curve incorrectly. It is very important to know how to place it correctly when you are drawing the curved line connecting the points that determine the shape of the armhole.

Drawing the armhole with the French curve is done in two stages: first, from the shoulder line to the upper chest line (Figure 61); and then from the upper chest line to the armhole line (Figure 62).

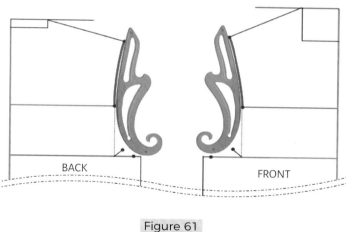

BACK   FRONT

Figure 61

Drawing the First Part of the Armhole

On both the back and the front, the armhole starts at the edge of the shoulder with the French curve positioned as shown in Figure 61.

This line takes a lightly rounded shape as it approaches the upper chest line.

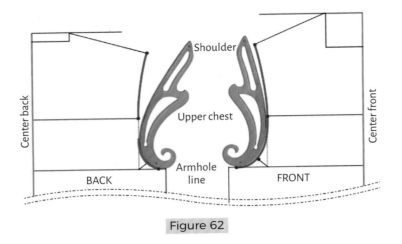

Figure 62

Drawing the Second Part of the Armhole

Because this part of the armhole is rounded, the French curve needs to be repositioned. Look for the position in which the curvature matches up (as in Figure 62). The drawing of the curve must absolutely pass through the reference points that were placed on the upper chest line, the flat area, and the armhole line.

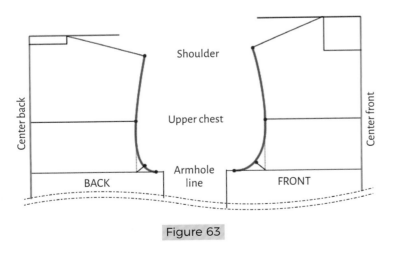

Figure 63

Be careful, though: for the flat area, the length of the bisecting line can change (see box, page 42).

BASIC DARTS

To reproduce the shape of a body on a flat pattern, you will have to absorb the extra volume created by the bust, the waist, and the shoulders. This is done by applying darts to the pattern. Every flat pattern includes these darts; then, when the pattern is manipulated, depending on the design to be created, they can be moved (or ignored, for instance, in the case of straight, loose clothing).

As a general rule, every basic pattern needs to include the following main darts:

- Back shoulder darts
- Front shoulder darts
- Waist darts

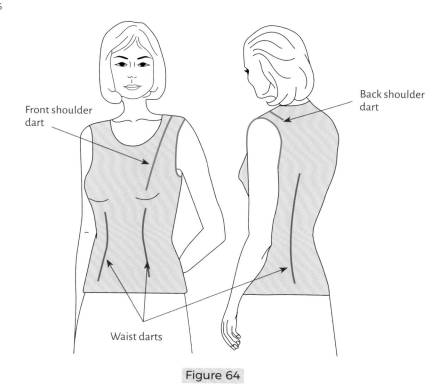

Front shoulder dart

Back shoulder dart

Waist darts

Figure 64

Note

To gain a good understanding of the role that each dart plays in the drafting of a basic pattern, follow the explanations given in the following pages methodically, because establishing the placement, height, and length of the darts is a crucial contributor to giving the garment a good drape and making it comfortable to wear.

BACK SHOULDER DART

In drafting patterns for bodices, this dart is often forgotten or ignored because it is very small: about 1 to 2 cm.

But leaving it out has a direct consequence that is out of proportion to its size: for a sleeveless garment, extra fabric at the armholes will form pleats (Figure 65B). Even the use of armhole facing or a bias to finish the armhole edge may not resolve this problem.

As for the case of a design with sleeves (Figure 65C), the extra fabric present due to the absence of the shoulder dart will drop toward the bottom edge of the armhole and, under the weight of the sleeve, visibly distort the draping of the fabric in the back, and sometimes the sleeve cap as well. For the sake of a good drape, apply this dart to the basic pattern.

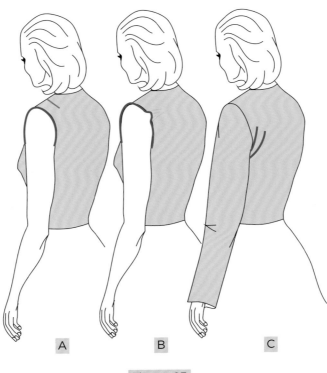

A   B   C

Figure 65

Different Placements of the Back Shoulder Dart

This small dart, essential for the construction of the garment, does not produce a very pleasing aesthetic effect when it is first positioned (Figure 65A). This is why it is often moved to a position that is less visible: to the armhole in the case of a princess seam (Figure 66), and otherwise to the center back seam.

Dart Moved to the Center Back

This adjustment is often used for tight-fitting clothes with a seam in the center back, such as suit jackets. The entire section that is affected by this modification will need to be shifted: the neckline, the shoulder line, and the armhole (in blue, Figure 67), to maintain the initial dimensions.

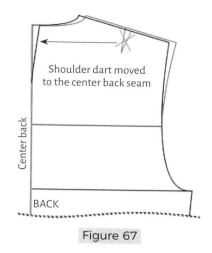

Shoulder dart moved to the center back seam

Center back

BACK

Figure 67

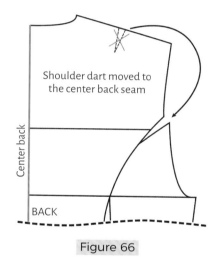

Shoulder dart moved to the center back seam

Center back

BACK

Figure 66

Dart Moved to the Armhole

If the design includes a seam that starts at the armhole and then joins the waist dart (called a princess seam), the shoulder dart can be moved to this seam (Figure 66). This seam is generally placed at the level of the upper chest line, for aesthetic reasons, but it can also be placed above or below the upper chest line, which will not change the construction. If you make this change, do not forget to adjust the lengths of the dart arms in the same way you adjusted the shoulder line (Figures 66 and 67, page 48). Then close up the dart and redraw the armhole curve.

47

Absorbing the Dart Width

If the design does not include a seam in either the armhole or the center back, the width of the dart can be absorbed into the length of the shoulder (Figure 68) in the front. This solution is often used in the construction and assembly of garments. This gives you two different shoulder lengths (back and front), but the adjustment of these two different lengths during assembly is easy to carry out, because the two shoulder edges are cut into the fabric on the false bias and stretch easily.

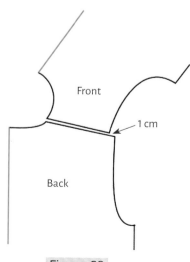

Front

1 cm

Back

Figure 68

Back Shoulder Dart Construction

In the middle of the shoulder length, draw a 7-cm long perpendicular line along the axis of the dart. Then establish a measurement of 1 cm on either side of that axis. To create the dart, draw a line from each of these reference points to the end of the axis of the dart.

The length and width measurements given here for darts are just indications; they will depend on the individual body shape. For example, in the case of a person with a rounded back, the width of the dart can be increased to 2 cm and its length shortened to 5 cm.

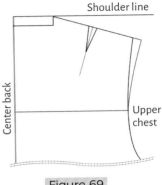

Figure 69

The measurements of this dart will then be correctly adjusted during fitting (see Figure 135, page 84). Because the width of the dart will be absorbed into the garment once the dart is closed up, the shoulder length needs to be restored to its original length. To make this happen, extend the end of the shoulder by the width of the dart (1 cm, if that is the measurement you used) (in blue, Figure 69). Then redraw the armhole line to match (in green, Figure 69) down to the upper chest line.

Adjusting the Shoulder Line

However long and wide the dart is, closing it up will distort the shoulder slope line along which it was placed (Figure 70). This line will have to be redrawn.

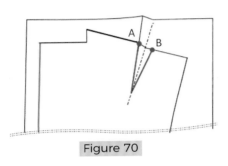

Figure 70

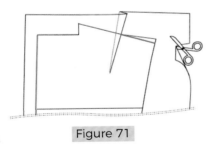

Figure 71

To do this, push the width of the dart toward the center front line by superimposing point A onto point B (Figure 70). Then, with the dart closed, redraw the shoulder slope line with a ruler, still adhering to the original angle of 18 degrees (green line, Figure 71). With the dart still closed up, cut the paper along the new line you have drawn.

> **Note**
>
> The construction of the flat pattern absolutely must include the back shoulder dart for the armhole drawing to be correct. This dart must not be forgotten or ignored under any circumstances.

FRONT SHOULDER DART

The role of the front shoulder dart, like that of the back shoulder dart (Figure 135, page 84), is to adjust the armhole so that it doesn't gape. It is absolutely essential to include this dart on the basic pattern, especially for fitted clothes.

The actual size of the front shoulder dart depends on the size of the full bust, and therefore on the measurement of the bust circumference. In drafting patterns based on standard measurements, we add 1 cm to the basic length, but in custom drafting, it is increased or decreased during the fitting process based on the size of the bust (Figure 134, page 83).

While it is positioned along the shoulder line to begin with, the front shoulder dart can be moved anywhere else around the bodice, depending on the seam being used or the design to be constructed (Figure 72). For more details about pivoting or moving the front shoulder dart, see the bodice adjustments (beginning on page 172).

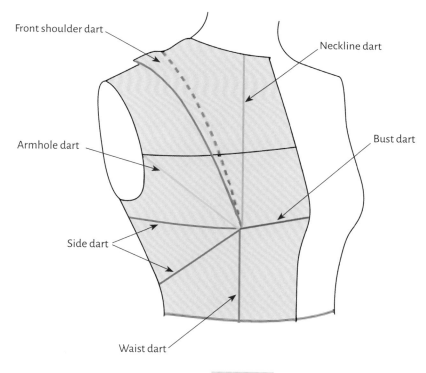

Figure 72

Front Shoulder Dart Construction

The second role that this dart plays is giving the fabric of the garment enough volume to cover the bust. To draft the front shoulder dart, you need the measurements of the bust length (see page 20), the bust-point-to-bust-point length (see page 21), and the bust circumference (see page 23).

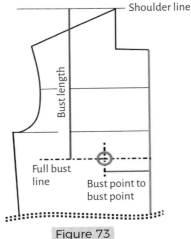

Figure 73

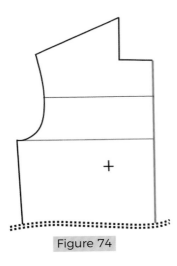

Figure 74

Starting anywhere along the shoulder line, draw a perpendicular line equal in length to the measurement of the bust length. Then draw a horizontal line to the center front: this is the bust line (black dotted line, Figure 73). Along this line (starting at the center front) go half the length of the bust-point-to-bust-point measurement and draw a short vertical line. The intersection of these two lines corresponds to the bust point (red circle, Figure 73).

To keep the pattern clear and easy to read, erase the lines that helped you determine the bust point, and leave only a small, clearly visible cross (Figure 74).

Checking the Draft

Before moving on to applying the darts, make sure that the drawings of the neckline and the shoulder slope correctly match the shape of the person whose measurements you have taken. Check using the auxiliary measurements and, if necessary, fix the drawing of the bodice before you add this dart. Because the application of the front shoulder dart will modify the shoulder line and the shape of the armhole curve, you will no longer be able to check this measurement later, and if you have made a mistake, you will be unable to continue with the construction.

Checking the Neckline Depth

In general, the measurements taken to draft the width and the depth of the neckline, starting at the base of the neck (Figure 27, page 22), are accurate if the pattern is drawn using standard measurements. But in the case of a pattern made to measure, the construction must match the person's shape.

To make this happen, transfer the height of the neckline depth, taken on the person (Figure 24, page 21) from the bust point to the center front, onto the pattern. If necessary, move the neckline depth up or down to adjust it (green lines, Figure 75).

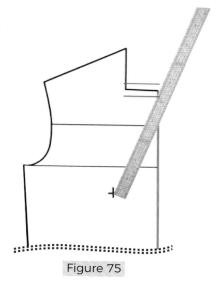

Figure 75

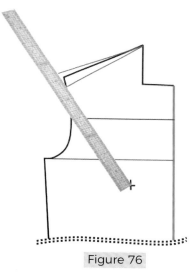

Figure 76

Checking the Shoulder Slope

The shoulder slope plays a very important role in the construction of the bodice: if the angle is too small, the armhole will gape, but if it is too large, it can make the front of the fabric shift to the side.

The 26-degree angle established for the shoulder slope on the front corresponds to the construction of standard patterns. But in custom drafting, you are strongly advised to include an additional measurement: the shoulder curve height (Figure 25, page 21).

On the pattern, take the shoulder curve height measured on the person and apply it to the line from the bust point to the acromion. If necessary, increase or decrease the slope (green lines, Figure 76).

Once you have verified the draft in this way, and made any necessary corrections, you can move to the following step: applying the front shoulder dart.

51

A Good Thing to Know

Once the corrections have been made on the pattern draft, erase the other lines that are no longer valid so as not to overload the pattern and to avoid possible confusion later on.

Width of the Front Shoulder Dart

Divide the length of the shoulder by 2 and place a dot at that middle point. Starting from that point, draw a straight line (green line, Figure 77) to the bust point (the little cross you drew previously, see Figures 73 and 74, page 50). The width of the front shoulder dart depends on the measurement of the bust circumference. It is equal to 1/20 of the bust circumference plus 1 cm. Along the shoulder line, and starting from the center point, measure the distance just calculated. Starting at the other end of the segment corresponding to this measurement, draw another straight line to the bust point (blue line, Figure 77).

Make the two arms of the dart (green and blue) equal, using the length of the first arm, drawn in green, as the length for both.

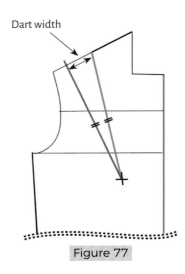

Dart width

Figure 77

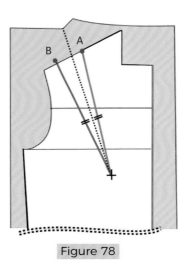

Figure 78

Closing the Dart

Close the front shoulder dart in such a way that the width of the dart is folded toward the center front: fold the paper along the line of the first arm of the dart (green line, Figure 78), then align the two arms of the dart (superimposing point A onto point B, Figure 78).

Reestablishing the Shoulder Line

Hold the dart closed, for instance with a pin or a piece of tape. Then, using a ruler, redraw the second half of the shoulder length (green line, Figure 79), maintaining the original angle of 26 degrees, the original slope of the shoulder line.

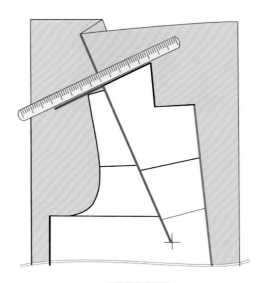

Figure 79

Reestablishing the Measurements

Unfold the front shoulder dart, then measure the dart widths along the upper chest line and the armhole line. Now reestablish these measurements, because when you closed the dart, the width of the front upper chest and the width of the upper part of the bodice will have become that much smaller. Do this by adding the two widths you have just measured to the two lines, starting from the curve of the armhole (blue arrows, Figure 80). Now redraw the new armhole curve by connecting points 1, 2, and 3 (Figure 81), maintaining the flat area of the armhole. This operation means that the widths of the upper chest and the armhole line will regain their original lengths after the dart is closed.

Remember that it is essential to build the front shoulder dart into the draft of the basic pattern for fitted or belted clothing designs.

On the other hand, for some clothing designs that are relaxed, wide, or made from stretchy fabric, this step is not necessary. In cases like that, we use the basic pattern as is (in black, Figure 81; see also page 89 for examples of the use of a basic pattern without darts).

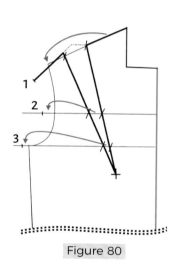

Figure 80

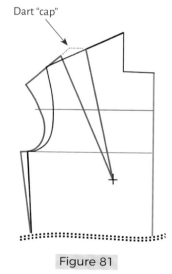

Dart "cap"

Figure 81

WAIST DARTS

In the same way that the front shoulder dart is used to adjust the armhole of the bodice, darts placed around the waist make it possible to adjust the garment at the waist.

This adjustment can be made by adding several darts, but the general rule is to stick to four main darts. In fact, if you don't follow this rule, you run the risk of throwing off the drape of the garment's fabric.

The first main dart placed at the waist is the front dart. Then come the two side darts, which will become one when the front and back are joined. The fourth dart, on the center back, is optional, and only used on certain kinds of design. The fifth dart is the one in the middle of the half-back.

The basic darts placed at the waist can be moved or changed during the modifications made to the basic pattern depending on the design (see the details of moving and altering beginning on page 172).

Placement of Waist Darts

The placement of the darts around the waist play an important role, both visually and for the garment's construction. The darts must be placed following the shape of the body, for instance the full bust shape on the front of the bodice pattern. On the back, on the other hand, placing them at regular distances provides a more esthetically pleasing result.

① **Front dart:** the placement of this dart depends on the length of the bust (page 20) and the bust-point-to-bust-point length (page 21). First draw a vertical line (dotted black line, Figure 82) downward from the bust point (black cross, Figures 82 and 83, page 50): this is the axis of this dart. Then, distribute the width of the dart to either side of the axis, half of it on each side.

② and ③ **Back and front side darts:** on the basic pattern, the lines and the width of the two side darts (front and back) will be identical. Thus, first draw the front side dart, then the back side dart as its mirror image. Sometimes, depending on the shape of the person or the garment design, these two darts will not be completely symmetrical.

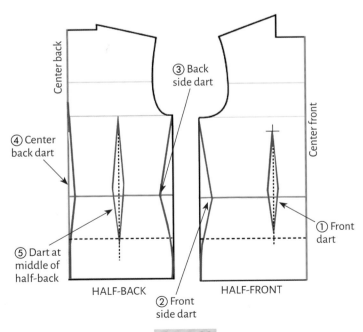

③ Back side dart

④ Center back dart

① Front dart

⑤ Dart at middle of half-back

② Front side dart

Center back · Center front · HALF-BACK · HALF-FRONT

Figure 82

④ **Center back dart:** this dart is applied when there is a seam in the middle of the back; it is only very rarely used for designs where the back is cut on the fold!

⑤ **Dart at middle of half-back:** this dart is placed in such a way as to create a nice visual effect in the middle of the half-back. To be able to draw this dart right, it is important to first place the side dart, then the center back dart (if there is one), and then, finally, to divide those two darts into two equal parts in order to be able to draw the corresponding axis in the middle of the half-back. Then the width of the dart is divided evenly on either side of the axis.

Width of the Waist Darts

A good drape for the garment also depends on the width absorbed by the waist darts.

The difference between the measurements of the full bust (page 50) and the waist must be distributed and absorbed regularly all around the waist, thanks to the use of darts. Every dart has to stay within certain limits in order to maintain the garment's vertical hang.

Front dart: The length of this dart should not be greater than 9 cm below the waistline, and its width should not be greater than 3 cm.

Side darts: Each of these darts should not be more than 4 cm wide; their lightly rounded shape ends at the level of the upper hips (page 61).

Center back dart: The width of this dart should not be greater than 1 to 2 cm; it is positioned between the armhole line and the upper hip line (dotted black line on the pattern back, Figure 83).

Middle of half-back dart: This dart should not be more than 11 cm long or below the waistline, and its width should not exceed 2 cm.

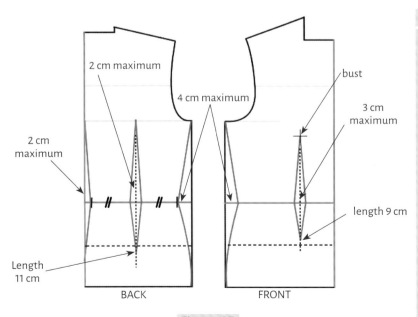

Figure 83

Calculating the Waist Dart Widths

The width of the darts placed at the waist is determined by the difference between the measurements of the various contours. The amount that needs to be absorbed at the waist, and thus the width of the darts, can be obtained in one of two ways: calculate either the difference between the measurement of the waist and that of the full bust, or else the difference between the measurement of the waist and that of the full hips. These two calculations do not yield the same number for the dart width. Thus, you need to know when and how to use one or the other of the calculation methods.

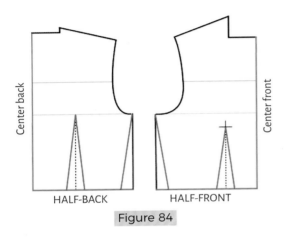

Figure 84

From the Full Bust to the Waist

For a garment pattern that stops at the waist (perfecto jacket, short vest, etc.), the question does not come up, since there are only two contour measurements in that case: the full bust and the waist (Figure 84). You just have to calculate the difference between the two. *For example, the full bust circumference is 88 cm and the waist circumference is 68 cm. In this case, the amount to be absorbed all around the waist is 88 minus 68, or 20 cm; per panel, the amount to be absorbed is 20 divided by 4 (5 cm). In other words, 5 cm on the half-front and 5 cm on the half-back.*

From the Full Bust to the Full Hips

For garments that go down all the way to the hips, there are three contour measurements: the full bust, the waist, and the full hips. The difference between the full bust circumference and the waist circumference is not the same as the difference between the waist circumference and the full hip circumference.

To understand this phase of the pattern drafting better, follow the steps of the calculation using the example of Figure 85.

For example, contour measurements: full bust circumference = 88 cm; waist circumference = 68 cm; full hip circumference = 92 cm. The difference between the bust and the waist is 88 minus 68, or 20 cm, to be absorbed at the waist. The difference between the full hip measurement and the waist is 92 minus 68, or 24 cm to be absorbed at the waist.

Depending on the method of calculation you use, then, you will obtain different measurements for the darts.

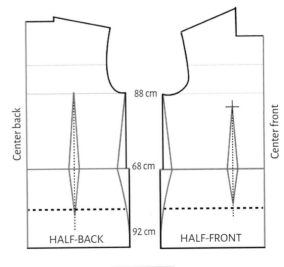

Figure 85

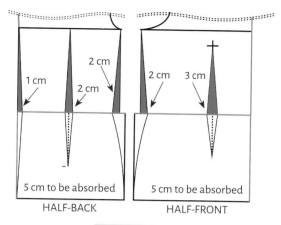

2 cm

1 cm

2 cm

2 cm 3 cm

5 cm to be absorbed

HALF-BACK

5 cm to be absorbed

HALF-FRONT

Figure 86

You can use either one of the two calculations, as long as you correctly place the measurements obtained onto the pattern draft; in other words, in the first case, you apply the measurements to the upper part of the bodice, and in the second case to the lower part. In both cases, you need to take a quarter of the total width that needs to be absorbed as the amount for the half-back.

Using the first calculation (difference between the full bust circumference and the waist circumference), you will obtain 20 divided by 4, or 5 cm. This corresponds to the dart width to be absorbed within each quarter of the pattern on the upper part (Figure 86).

Using the second calculation (difference between the full hip circumference and the waist circumference), you will obtain 24 divided by 4, or 6 cm. This corresponds to the dart width to be absorbed within each quarter of the pattern on the lower part (Figure 87).

In both cases, you will end up with the same pattern (Figures 86 and 87), but the dart values will be applied differently.

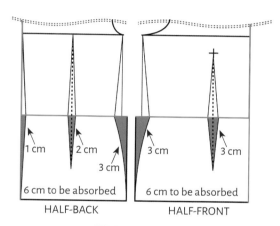

1 cm

2 cm

3 cm

3 cm

3 cm

6 cm to be absorbed

HALF-BACK

6 cm to be absorbed

HALF-FRONT

Figure 87

Remember

If the contour difference is calculated between the full bust and the waist, apply the dart widths starting at the side line in the upper part of the bodice (green darts, Figure 86). On the other hand, if the contour difference is calculated between the full hips and the waist, apply the dart widths starting at the side line in the lower part of the bodice (blue darts, Figure 87).

Additional Darts at the Waist

If the amount that needs to be absorbed at the waist is large, it will be necessary to use an additional dart. Additional darts on the back and the front are about 2 cm shorter than the main darts (Figure 88).

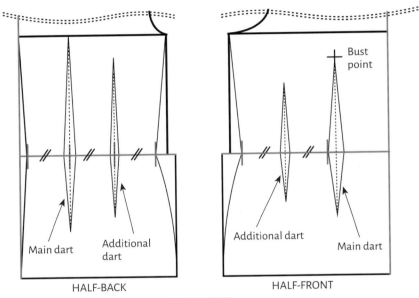

Main dart   Additional dart

HALF-BACK

Bust point

Additional dart   Main dart

HALF-FRONT

Figure 88

Additional Dart in the Back: Divide the distance between the arm of the side dart and the arm of the center back dart by 3, draw the axes of the darts at the points of those thirds (blue reference lines, Figure 88), then apply the widths of the darts evenly on either side of each axis.

Front: Divide the distance between the arm of the dart positioned under the bust point and the arm of the side dart by 2, then apply the widths of the darts evenly on either side of the axis.

Applying the
Flat Areas of the Darts

A garment needs to follow the shape of the body, and thus it is necessary to apply a flat area to the waist by drawing the shape of the dart at that spot. This small flat distance varies from body to body, depending on how well-defined the waist is. In general, the flat area of the darts at the waist is about 2 to 4 cm long. If the dart is wide (for example 3 cm), this flat area will be 2 cm long; if the dart is only 1 or 1.5 cm, the flat area will be 3 cm long or longer.

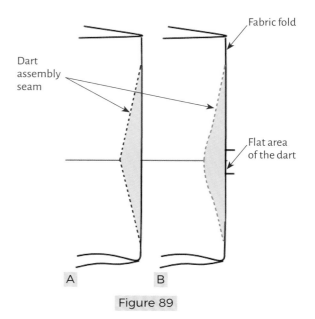

Figure 89

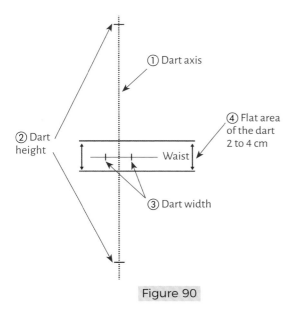

Figure 90

There is also a technical reason for applying this flat area. The dart assembly seam is automatically rounded along the waistline (Figure 89B): When you're sewing on a machine, it is not a good idea to sew in a straight line right up to the waistline (Figure 89A) and then stop the machine, turn the garment, and sew in another straight line to the end of the dart.

During the sewing, this flat area is applied without reference points: there is no mark on the fabric, and there is only the width of the dart to go by. On the pattern draft, on the other hand, the length of the flat area is applied.

① On the waistline, first draw the axis of the dart.
② Determine the height of the dart and indicate its endpoints.
③ Now indicate the width of the dart.
④ Indicate the length of the flat area, distributed equally above and below the waistline.

Shape of the Waist Darts

Take a ruler and align it along the points marking the height and the width of the dart, then draw a straight line (green line, Figure 91A) to the line that indicates the flat area of the dart (black line, Figure 91A). Repeat this operation on both sides of the width of the dart, both above and below the waistline.

The two arms of the dart, stopped at the width of the flat area, are now connected by a lightly curved line. To do this, position the French curve in such a way that it can connect the upper arms and the lower arms of the dart, passing through the point on the waistline that indicates the width of the dart (Figure 91B).

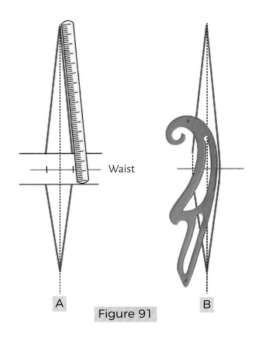

Figure 91

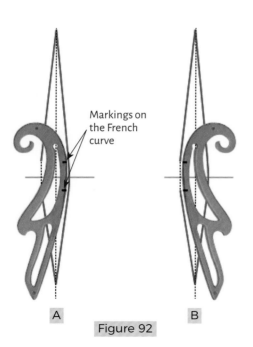

Markings on the French curve

Figure 92

To make sure that the shape of the dart is identical on both sides of the axis, when you draw the flat area of the first arm of the dart, make marks on the edge of the French curve to indicate the width of the flat area (Figure 92A). When you turn the French curve around to finish drawing the second arm of the dart, line up the markings indicating the width of the flat area with the ends of the straight lines of the dart (Figure 92B).

Shape of the Side Dart

This dart, positioned along the side line of the bodice, is drawn in the same way as the darts positioned along the waist on the front or the back. Start by marking the width of the dart along the waistline and then mark the length of the flat area, equally distributed above and below the waistline (Figure 93; see also Figure 90, page 59).

Then, with the help of a ruler, draw the top part of the dart by connecting the edge of the armhole along the side line with the line of the flat area, aligned with the reference point marking the width of the dart (green line, Figure 94).

The next step is to draw the part below the waist, down to the full hip line. The shape of this line is not the same for the bodice and for the skirt. In the case of the bodice, the curve is flattened, to avoid producing a "beak" along the side during assembly. To do this, position the French curve as in Figure 95.

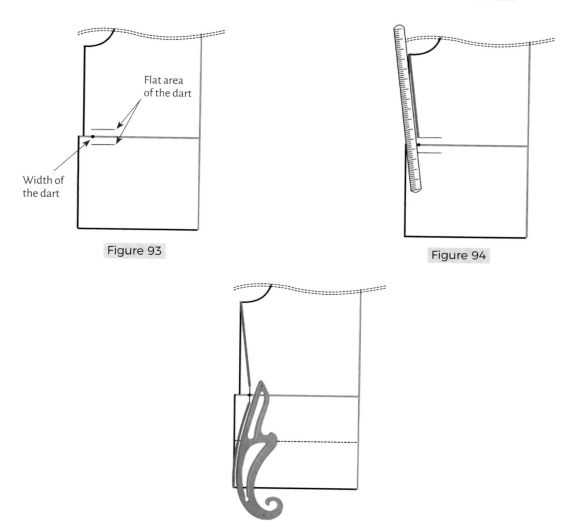

Flat area
of the dart

Width of
the dart

Figure 93

Figure 94

Figure 95

The two lines of the dart (above and below), which are stopped at the level of the width of the flat area at the waist, are connected by a slightly rounded line. Position the French curve in such a way as to connect the upper and lower lines of the dart, passing through the point placed on the waistline to indicate the width of the dart.

At the level of the waistline, the dart line is almost straight, and then it rejoins the side line below the upper hip line with a light curve (Figure 96).

Figure 97 shows the position that should not be used under any circumstances.

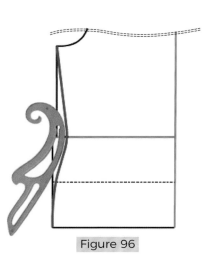

Figure 96

Incorrect

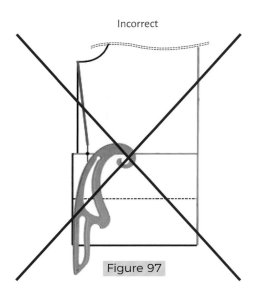

Figure 97

Remember

On the pattern drawn for the bodice, the widths of the side darts are identical, and the widths of the front and back are divided evenly on either side of the axis. To make the work easier and avoid making mistakes, indicate the length of the flat area on the edge by tracing its shape on the front (Figure 92, page 60). Then, by turning the French curve over to make a mirror image and placing those marks at the ends of the dart's straight lines, you will obtain a curve that is strictly identical for the back.

SHAPE OF THE NECKLINE

It is hard to draw the shape of the neckline correctly by drawing the curve of the back neckline and the curve of the front neckline separately.

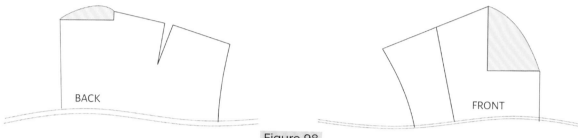

Figure 98

To make the drawings match up as they should, start by tracing the upper parts of the bodice, back and front, following the traced shoulder slope (Figure 98, in green). Cut them out leaving a large margin on the paper for the necklines (Figure 98, in brown).

Then position these front and back parts of the pattern next to each other, making sure to make the back and front shoulder lines match up correctly, up to the darts (Figure 98, green).

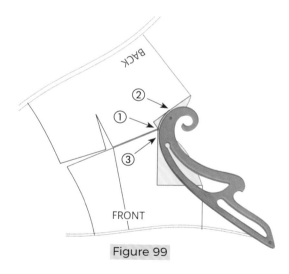

Figure 99

Back Neckline Shape

The curve of the back neckline includes a rather wide flat area, starting at the center back. The flat area is rarely formed along the depth of the neckline at the end of the shoulder. In order not to cut the neckline too deep, the French curve must be positioned correctly.

Place the curved edge approximately at the middle of the width of the back neckline (point 2, Figure 99) and make it touch the edge of the shoulder (point 1, Figure 99). On the front, the French curve needs to follow the vertical line of the neckline for 2 to 3 cm (point 3, Figure 99). The placement of the French curve will depend on the measurements and the body shape.

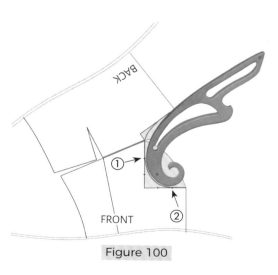

Figure 100

Front Neckline Shape

The shape of the neckline should not be too low-cut, either. After all, it is easier to cut away the surplus during the fitting than to try to add back what is missing.

In general, the flat areas of the neckline should make up about a third of the width (point 1, Figure 100) and a third of the depth (point 2, Figure 100) of the neckline.

Position the French curve in such a way that its edges touch the reference points, as shown in Figure 100, then draw the front neckline.

As with the back, the shape and the lengths of the flat areas along the height and width of the neckline depend on the measurements and the body shape.

The neckline should be continuous all around the back and front (blue line). Then cut away the margin of the paper (in brown), following the neckline (Figure 101).

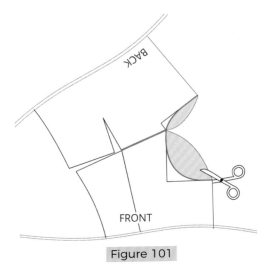

Figure 101

CHECKING THE ARMHOLE

Correcting the Shape of the Armhole

Close up the front shoulder dart and the back shoulder dart, then adjust the two shoulder lines as shown in Figure 102. The back and front armhole contours should follow a line that is lightly curved but continuous, without any "beaks" (red circle, Figure 103) or hollows.

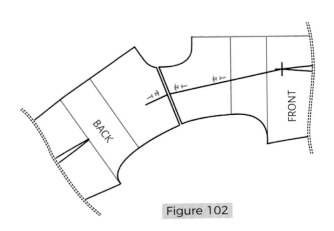

Figure 102

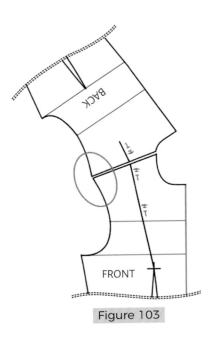

Figure 103

Correcting the Armhole Line

If the armhole line is not continuous and includes any rupture in the curve (Figure 103), it needs to be redrawn with the help of a French curve, as in Figure 104, making sure to respect the widths of the front and back upper chest lines.

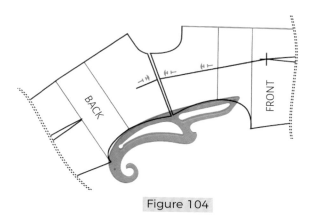

Figure 104

Correcting the Armhole Length

After adjusting the armhole shape, it is essential to check the lengths of the back and front armholes separately. In principle, if the armhole is well constructed, there should be a difference of 2 cm between the two lengths. Depending on the body shape, the back can be longer than the front—or the opposite. But if this difference is greater than 1 to 2 cm, the construction needs to be checked, either on the flat pattern or during the fitting, and it needs to be corrected if necessary.

An error at this level can make it hard or even impossible to position the sleeve cap in the armhole, and it would disrupt the drape of the sleeve. This is often due to an error in the shoulder slope line or in how the measurement of the full bust circumference is distributed between the back and the front.

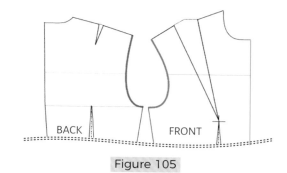

Figure 105

BASIC ENLARGEMENT

The body measurements used to draft the pattern match the exact outline of the body. To be able to pull the garment over the bust and make any potential corrections, it is necessary to add the basic enlargements to the height and width (green lines, Figure 106).

This enlargement corresponds, essentially, to the width of the fabric and the space taken up by the seam allowances.

In general, these allowances are also only added to the fitting pattern.

The enlargements added to the garment can vary according to the style of the garment (tailored, athletic, casual), the particular design, the thickness of the fabric, comfort, and finally, individual preferences.

Here is how to add the basic enlargements to the draft of the fitting pattern.

① Draw a line parallel to the shoulder line, 2 cm above it (blue lines).
② Lower the armhole line by 2 cm using a parallel straight line (blue lines).
③ Along the line drawn in step 2, starting at the side line, measure 1 cm on both the back and the front. Then, from these points, draw lines parallel to the side lines (green lines, Figure 107).

Now redraw the armhole curve starting from the upper chest line: 1 cm on the original pattern + 1 cm of enlargement. To keep this curve from being distorted, trace it and then offset it by adjusting it to the point of the upper chest line.

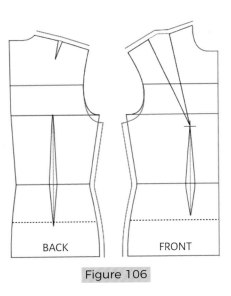

Figure 106

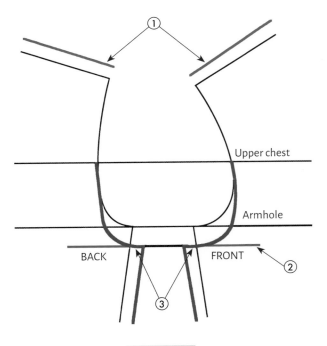

Figure 107

SEAM ALLOWANCES

Every pattern has seam allowances. They are usually 1 cm wide, but they might vary according to different needs. On the fitting pattern, the seam allowance on the side is wider: 2 to 3 cm (for instance), in order to make any necessary corrections to the side line (page 82). Thus, add the seam allowances to the back and front (dotted black lines, Figure 108), taking the enlargement lines into account (in green).

Depending on the design, the back can be drafted and then cut into the fabric in two different ways.

A **With a center back dart.** The back, cut in two steps, has to include the assembly seam in the middle. Thus, the seam allowance must be added at the center back.

B **Without a center back dart.** The back is cut by placing the middle of it on the fabric fold; this is called cutting on the fold. A pattern drafted to be cut on the fold has no seam allowance at the center back.

However, for a fitting pattern, the back is always cut on the fold, even if the design has a center back dart (Figure 108B). The center back seam cut in this way will not get in the way during a fitting for making any potential corrections and will not create any thickness along this length.

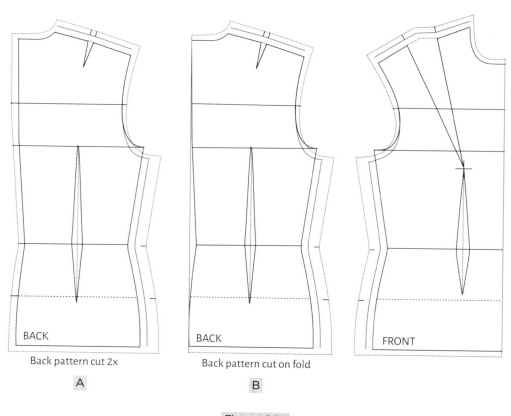

BACK

BACK

FRONT

Back pattern cut 2x

Back pattern cut on fold

A

B

Figure 108

FINISHED FITTING PATTERN

Every pattern includes the essential instructions for cutting:

- Straight-grain or cross-grain
- Notches to help with assembly
- Instructions for how to position the pattern

  On the fold: Indicates which part of the pattern should be positioned on the fold of the fabric. Cutting on the fold makes it possible to obtain perfectly symmetrical pieces: for example, the center back line may be placed on the fold.

  2X (twice): This indicates that the pattern is placed on top of two layers of fabric that are cut together in order to obtain two identical pieces.

- The overlap, about 2 to 3 cm from the center front line, to make it possible to close the front.

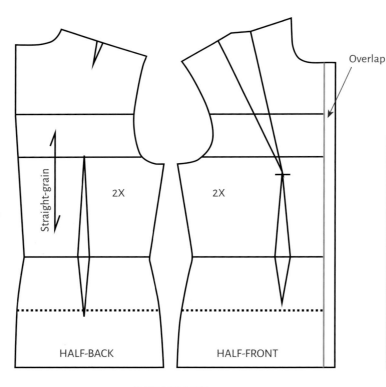

Figure 109

Note

On a fitting pattern, you must retain the dart markings on the fabric to be able to easily make any necessary corrections to the darts, such as moving them, enlarging them, or reducing them.

CUTTING

To correctly adjust the fitting pattern to the shape and sizes of the figure for which it was drafted, it has to be cut out of a woven fabric. This fabric cannot be too thick or too rigid. On the other hand, you should also not choose a fabric that is elastic, fluid, or that stretches easily, because that will distort the result. The ideal fabric is the muslin fabric used for draping.

PLACEMENT OF THE FITTING PATTERN

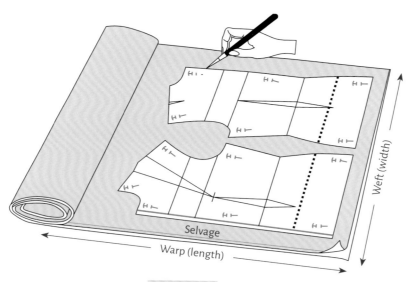

Figure 110

Double the fabric over so that you can cut the two half-fronts and the two half-backs, left and right sides, at the same time. It is very important to respect the straight-grain indication on the pattern, which is parallel to the selvage of the fabric. Then pin the pattern to the fabric at several points (Figure 110). Trace the outline of the pattern onto the fabric using a tool designed for that, such as a colored pencil or a piece of chalk.

Note

When you transfer the pattern onto the fabric, do not forget to transfer the notches and the reference points for positioning the construction lines; these will be necessary for applying any necessary corrections to the fabric later.

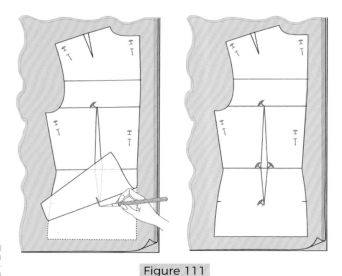
Figure 111

INDICATING THE DART WIDTHS

On the fitting pattern, the basic darts are drawn: front shoulder dart, back shoulder dart, and waist dart. Thus, their widths and shapes must be transferred from the pattern to the fabric.

To do this, poke a pin into the end of the dart (Figure 111), making sure it goes through both the paper and the fabric, then lift the paper slightly so that the pin stays in place and slide your pencil underneath in order to mark this placement with a small dot on the fabric. Repeat this operation at each of the points that demarcate the width and length of the dart. It is not necessary at this point to connect those dots with straight lines, because the darts may be adjusted and corrected during the fitting of the fabric.

BEFORE CUTTING THE FABRIC

Remove the paper pattern and pin the two layers of fabric together at several different places inside the outline, so that they will not move during the cutting and to secure them for the transfer of any reference marks made later. Check very carefully that all the reference marks from the paper pattern have been transferred to the fabric: the notches, the points that correspond to the placement of the darts, the reference lines, and the construction lines (center, waist, upper chest... Figure 112).

Cut the fabric following the outline of the bodice, and don't forget to make notches (about 3 to 5 mm from the edge) according to the reference marks.

The points that indicate the outline of the darts and the placement of the lines should be transferred to the second half-piece of the back and of the front. To do this, poke the pin into a point that has already been marked, pass through the two layers of fabric, and mark the exit point of the pin on the other side with a pencil. Repeat this step until each of the two pieces of fabric (top and bottom) has all the same markings.

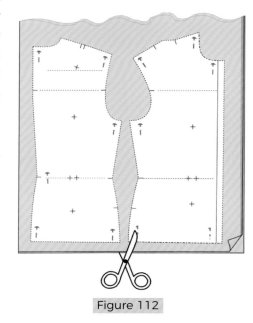
Figure 112

ASSEMBLY AND FITTING

ASSEMBLY

As we have seen in the previous pages, it is necessary, to obtain an accurate and well-fitting basic pattern, to proceed in a very precise and careful manner.

Once the fitting pattern has been made, we can move to the next step: assembling the muslin, then proceeding to a fitting to find and adjust any potential imperfections in the construction.

There are several ways to assemble the elements of the bodice cut into the muslin. In practice, every technique is good to the extent that it produces satisfactory results, does not complicate the job of making adjustments, and makes it easy to correct the basic pattern.

The technique presented here is the one most frequently used because it is simple, efficient, clear, and yields a clean result.

A Good Thing to Know

Do not use a sewing machine to put together the fitting bodice. If you do that, it will be hard to make any necessary corrections, because the relevant seams will have to be unstitched, which is a long and relatively complicated job.

FITTING

The fitting is the culmination of all the work you have done so far: it is strongly suggested that you fully understand and very carefully carry out the following instructions.

ASSEMBLING THE FITTING BODICE

The assembly method presented here, validated by many experienced pattern makers, produces a very clean, neat result and makes corrections easy, because it is simple to see a potential problem. If the dart widths need to be enlarged or reduced, for example, you can move the pins directly on the figure. This method also allows you to easily redraw the lines and the edges of the seam allowances, because they are placed on the inside and thus do not get in the way of the adjustment work. Equally important is the fact that you can see how the thickness of the fabric responds at the seam allowances in terms of width and height.

Note

It requires a certain amount of experience to master this technique. At first, it is hard to keep the pinning regular and to achieve a consistent width in the pressed edges.

APPLYING THE ASSEMBLY TECHNIQUE

In the fitting pattern assembly technique presented here, the seam allowances are always pressed back, held in place by pins that are positioned at an angle to the edges of the fabric fold. Make sure that the points of the pins used in the assembly are always pointing downward, the pinhead pointing up: this is a safety issue.

① Place one of the pieces to be assembled on a flat surface (such as a table), then fold the seam allowance of the second piece according to the intended width and lay it on top of the seam allowance of the first piece. Poke a pin just into the crease of the folded allowance.

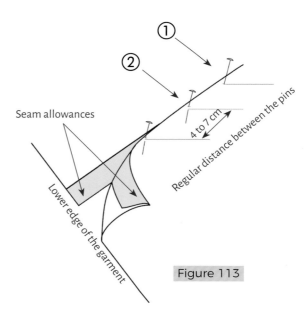

Seam allowances

Lower edge of the garment

Regular distance between the pins

4 to 7 cm

Figure 113

②Place the pins at an angle of approximately 45 degrees, poking about 2 to 3 mm of fabric. Space the pins evenly (about 4 to 7 cm apart). They should not be spaced too far apart, nor too close together, for fear of overloading the edges.

ORDER OF ASSEMBLY

The muslin fitting bodice is made up of three pieces: the back and the two parts of the front. As with a classical garment assembly, it is important to respect the order of the steps to make the work easier and get an accurate result. For example, if you pinned the sides and shoulders first, you would not be able to get to the waist darts easily to close them.

Thus, it is strongly suggested that you scrupulously follow the assembly steps for the fitting bodice presented in these pages.

To begin with, close up all the darts, first the front shoulder darts, then the back shoulder darts, then the waist darts. Then, close up the sides, and finally, the shoulders.

Note

On one hand, it is important not to place the pins parallel to the edge of the fabric fold, and on the other hand, not to take more than 2 to 3 mm of fabric thickness with the pin. Otherwise, the assembly will lose its flexibility and will not relax, and this temporary seam runs the risk of pulling, because it is fixed in place by the pins.

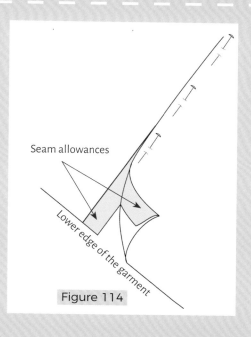

Seam allowances

Lower edge of the garment

Figure 114

Closing the Waist Darts

When assembling the fitting bodice, you must always begin by closing the width of the dart along the waistline, then close it along its length (Figure 115). The margin (the fold) of this dart must be pressed toward the center. Pin all of the darts placed along the waist line, in both the front and the back, in this way.

Figure 115

Closing the Front Shoulder Dart

The front shoulder dart must be closed starting from the shoulder line. The head of the dart drawn during the drafting of the pattern (see page 53) allows you to respect the slope of the shoulder and the width of the front shoulder dart. Align the edges of the width of the dart and insert the first pin (Figure 116). The margin of this dart is pressed toward the center front.

Then, laying the dart's width lines on top of each other, pin the length of the dart, placing the pins every 4 to 5 cm. Build in a flat area of about 2 cm on the bust.

Note

Once the front shoulder dart is closed, the shoulder line should be nice and straight. Use a ruler to make sure that this is indeed the case (Figure 116). If necessary, it can be corrected, maintaining the angle of 26 degrees (pages 41 and 52).

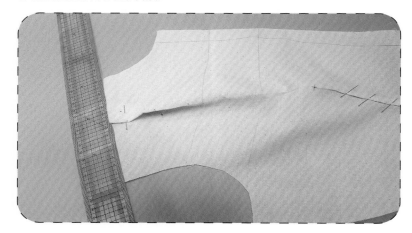

Figure 116

Flat Area at the Bust

The front shoulder dart and the waist dart create a continuous line on the front outline (Figure 64, page 45). But in actuality, this line is interrupted by the curve of the bust—otherwise, these two closed-up darts would come together to a point. To avoid the formation of this "beak" at the level of the bust point, the two darts must be separated by a space of about 2 cm between the end of each of the darts to create a flat area there. The exact size of the flat area depends on the size of the bust, and thus you will have to adjust depending on the specific figure.

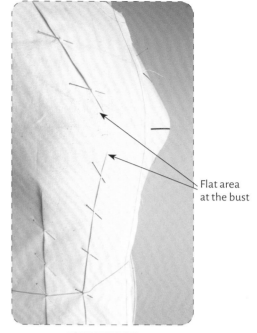

Flat area at the bust

Figure 117

Closing the Back Shoulder Dart

As with the front shoulder dart, we start closing the width of the back shoulder dart at the shoulder line. Because the width and length of this dart are very small, the pinning must be very precise. As with the front shoulder dart, use a ruler to make sure that the shoulder line is nice and straight once the shoulder dart has been closed up (Figure 118).

Figure 118

Figure 119

Side Seam Allowances

The side line is made up of two parts that have different shapes. The first part, from the armhole line to the waist, is a straight line; thus, you will have no problem pinning it. The second part, from the waist to the full hips, is lightly rounded, because of the shape of the hips; thus, this piece will be harder to put together correctly. To make the assembly easier and to preserve a regular seam allowance width that is identical on both sides, it is strongly recommended to use an iron to mark the 1 cm fold along the edge of the side of the back (Figure 119).

Closing Up the Sides

As with the waist darts, start this assembly from the waistline. Place the front on a flat surface, then lay the previously indicated fold (along the edge of the side of the back) on top of the edge of the side of the front, maintaining the width of the seam allowance. Insert a first pin to connect the waistlines of the two sides. Then match up the two armhole curves (Figure 120) and place several more pins at regular intervals from the armhole line to the waist.

The assembly of the lower part of the bodice is more delicate, because you have to be very careful not to flatten the rounded shape of the line. During assembly, frequently check to make sure that the seam allowance is maintained at the intended width and that the two edges (front and back) are well-aligned. Start the assembly of the side on the lower part of the bodice starting at the waist, and pin gradually down toward the bottom.

Figure 120

Closing the Shoulders

This final step in assembling the fitting bodice is quite delicate. The method used for assembling the bodice (pins placed along the edge of a fold) assumes that the back shoulder fold is overlaid onto the front shoulder edge (the shoulder seam allowance pressed toward the back). This automatically means that the back muslin is underneath the shoulder assembly line. In positioning the pins, therefore, there is the risk that you will include the back fabric in the assembly seam.

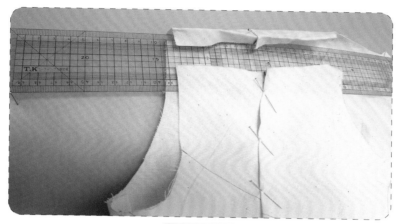

Figure 121

To make this job easier, position the bodice in such a way that the back armhole is accurately overlaid onto the front armhole. The shoulder seam allowance is pressed toward the back, thus the fold of this allowance needs to have been prepared ahead of time (Figure 121).

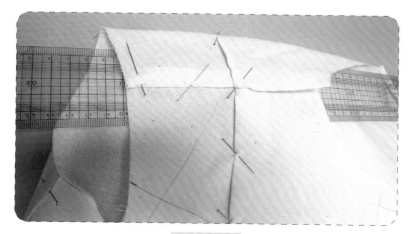

Figure 122

Now, place a ruler between the two layers of fabric (Figure 121) and start the assembly by lining up the fold of the back shoulder dart with the fold of the front shoulder dart. Lay the back fold over the front one, maintaining the 1 cm margin. Then, connect the two shoulder lengths: back and front from the armhole to the neckline (Figure 122).

FITTING THE BODICE

This task must be carried out with the utmost care and precision. During this step, you will doubtless encounter problems with the adaptation of the pattern, connected to the shape of the person for whom the bodice was made. But for every problem that appears during the fitting of the muslin, there is an appropriate solution.

The basic muslin pattern is the imprint of the body; the fitting must be done on the figure when it is dressed very lightly (for instance, a thin fabric tank top) and without sleeves, so that the thickness of what the figure is wearing will not give you incorrect feedback.

The fitting and then the alterations presented in this chapter are basic to creating made-to-measure garments and allow you to correct all the many mistakes or imperfections in the pattern, most of which will be addressed in these pages.

During the fitting, the most important issue is how the fabric of the bodice drapes: in other words, all of the vertical lines drawn on the fitting bodice (center back and front, side line, dart axes...) need to fall straight down, perfectly aligning with the lines of the mannequin.

Note

To make the problems and then their solutions easy to see, the fitting is shown here on a mannequin.

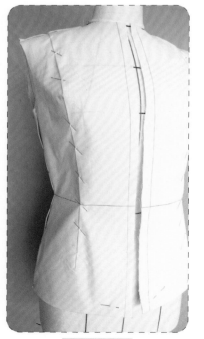

Figure 123

CENTER FRONT

Put the bodice on the mannequin without closing the front and observe how the two edges of the front fall: they should be nice and vertical, and they should match up: there should not be any gap nor any overlap between them. If they do match up as they should, that means that the shoulder slope and the width of the front shoulder dart were properly calculated and applied and that they correspond to the figure's shape.

This first assessment of the bodice is essential. If the center front drapes well, you may still have some minimal and simple corrections to make to the bodice as a whole to finalize it. On the other hand, if it does not drape well, then most of the time you will have to correct the shoulder slope, the width and length of the darts, or the side line, by moving it slightly toward the back or the front, starting at the waist in the lower part of the bodice.

THE BODICE

78

Correcting a Gap Between the Two Half Center-Fronts

The main causes of a gap between the two edges of the front, on the lower or upper part of the bodice, are an incorrect shoulder slope, front shoulder dart width, or front length.

First, check whether, on the flat pattern, the measurement taken from the figure (Figure 20, page 20) does indeed correspond to the length transferred to the pattern (Figure 49, page 35, step 10). If the two measurements do not correspond, then it is imperative that you correct the flat pattern and cut out a new front and then reassemble it with the rest of the pattern.

If the measurements are accurate, then the shoulder slope must be corrected: in this case, the angle applied to the basic flat pattern (front—26 degrees and back—18 degrees, page 41) do not correspond to the shape of the figure and must be changed.

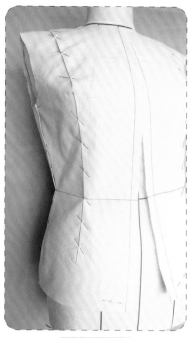

Figure 124

Changing the slope

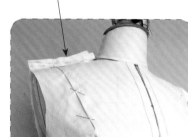

Corrected center front

Figure 125

Changing the Shoulder Slope

Remove the pins that are keeping the shoulders together, then move the front part slightly upward while seeing how the center line drawn on the bodice reacts (Figure 123). When it falls vertically, anchor this position by pinning the small fold on the shoulder (Figure 125). Be careful, because when you lift the shoulder, the neckline will also move up, and you will have to mark the new neckline depth (Figure 127).

When you make this correction, it creates a small surplus of fabric along the shoulder length. Now repin it the way it should be, then take the garment off the mannequin to redraw the correct neckline depth lines and shoulder slope lines on the muslin while it's flat.

This doesn't always happen, but it's possible that, because of the correction, the shoulder length may now not be long enough. If this happens, add a small piece of fabric and assemble it lying flat so as not to produce the thickness of a seam allowance (Figure 108, page 67). Then restore the shoulder length and slope.

Figure 126

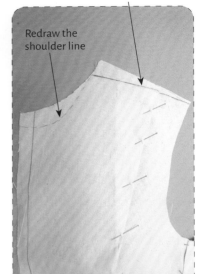

Redraw the neckline

Redraw the shoulder line

Figure 127

Note

Making sure to get a good drape of the center front during the fitting of the bodice is a tremendously important, very precise, and rather complex task. But all of the following adjustments of the muslin to fit the shape of the figure depend on this step.

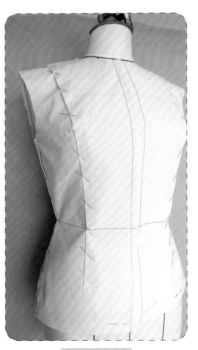

Figure 128

Verifying the Front Drape

Of course, you can't just fix one side of the bodice. You will have to apply the same corrections on the second shoulder. Then put the corrected bodice back on the mannequin.

Once again, observe how the two center lines fall: If their drape is nice and vertical and the edges do not gap along either the upper or lower part of the bodice, then go on to the next step of the fitting.

Otherwise, repeat the previous step until you obtain a satisfactory result.

BACK OF THE BODICE

As a general rule, the drape of the back of the fitting bodice, which depends on whether the center back line falls straight, is always right. It is very rare for it not to fall vertically the way it should. This line can only be disrupted if the two shoulders do not have the same slope or if the widths of the seam allowance have not been maintained during the assembly.

Using waist darts at the center back is not necessary for all designs, but on a fitting bodice, where the enlargements are minimal, these darts are essential and must be established so that the muslin will follow the shapes of the body nicely—otherwise, the fabric will gape at the waist. The dart width is 1 cm on standard patterns, but here you will have to adapt that depending on the person's shape.

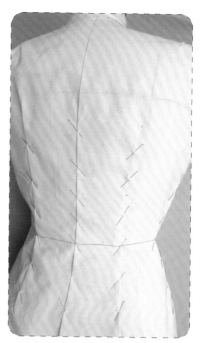

Figure 129

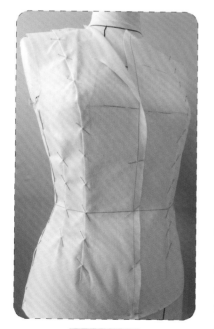

Figure 130

FRONT WAIST DARTS

The next step in the fitting is to check the placement of the front darts. To do this, close up the front by covering up the overlaps in such a way that the vertical line of the center front of the right side of the bodice is accurately superimposed onto the vertical line of the center front of the left side of the bodice. Pin it together, starting at the waist, to match up the horizontal lines of the two sides of the bodice. Then, in the same way, align the armhole lines, the upper chest lines, the upper hip lines, and the full hip lines. During the construction of the bodice pattern, you will have applied either one (page 54) or two (page 58) darts, depending on your calculations, but during the fitting of the bodice, these darts can be moved or eliminated, depending on the body shape. The dart placement should be such that they do not produce folds, and the muslin should lie flat against the bodice. If this is not the case, take out the existing darts and establish new ones that work with the shape of the figure.

THE SIDE LINE

The drape of the side line should not be checked and corrected until the bodice has been closed up, after the drape of the center front and center back has been verified.

The side line, like all the vertical lines of the fitting pattern, must have a perfectly vertical drape on the figure seen in profile (Figure 131), even if, in actuality, it includes rounded forms produced by the hips and the waist darts.

Sometimes this line tilts toward the front or toward the back; this tilt usually begins starting at the waist-line and going downward and is a function of the size of the buttocks—or, more rarely, the size of the belly. This effect does not mean that the basic construction was badly done or that you did your calculations incorrectly; instead, this is a result of a very particular body shape.

Starting from where the line no longer follows the vertical drape, mark the correct placement of the line with a wax pencil (B2, for example), without worrying about the assembly seam of the back with the front. Take out the pins along as much of the length as is necessary, then add a strip of fabric on the side of the line where the width is missing to restore the vertical line—either on the back or on the front. This addition of fabric should be assembled flat so that it does not add extra volume or thickness (Figure 132).

Figure 131

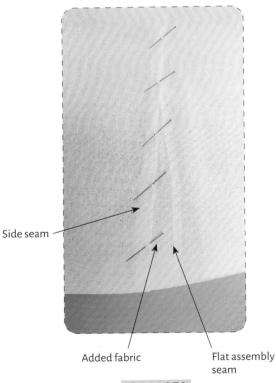

Side seam

Added fabric

Flat assembly seam

Figure 132

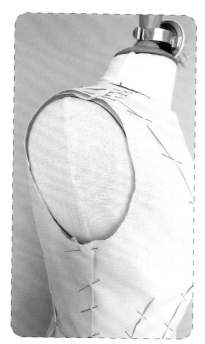

Figure 133

ARMHOLE

This step in the corrections is extremely important. An armhole that does not match the body shape will create extra fabric underneath the arm, which will produce folds (Figure 65, page 46) and a distorted sleeve drape during assembly.

A correctly constructed armhole needs to be well-adjusted all around the arm. This depends entirely on the widths assigned to the front shoulder dart and the back shoulder dart. During the drafting of a flat pattern using standard measurements, the width would correspond to 1/20th of the circumference of the full bust + 1 cm (see page 49). But when creating a pattern to measure, it needs to be adapted to the size of the bust.

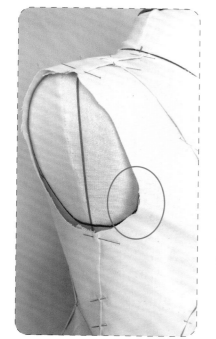

Figure 134

Correcting the Front Armhole

Gaping along the lower part of the armhole is often a result of using an inadequate width for the front shoulder dart; less often, it results from poor assembly (failing to maintain the width of the seam allowance).

To fix this problem, the width of the front shoulder dart needs to be increased. To do this, remove the pins that have been placed along the shoulder line and the pins along the length of the dart; then add to the amount folded into the dart until all of the extra fabric along the armhole has been absorbed. Now pin the new width of the front shoulder dart (a measurement that you will have to transfer to the flat pattern later, see page 85). Because this operation will throw off the shoulder line, retrace and readjust the shoulder line (Figure 79, page 52) after you have closed the dart.

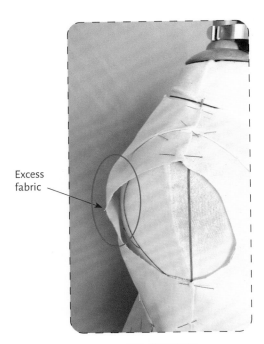

Excess fabric

Figure 135

Correcting the Back Armhole

The back shoulder dart plays the same role as the front shoulder dart: It is used to adjust all of the fabric of the half-curve of the armhole all around the arm. On a standard pattern, this dart is about 1 cm wide, but in reality it depends on the shape and size of the rounding of the back and the curve of the shoulders, which vary from one body shape to another.

To remove the excess fabric that is visible in the form of a gaping in the edge of the armhole, proceed in the same way as for the front armhole: Increase the width of the shoulder dart, then restore the original armhole curve (Figure 120, page 76) and the shoulder line (Figure 71, page 48).

Note

It is not recommended to adjust the armhole and the center front drape at the same time, even if both require increasing the width of the front shoulder dart or back shoulder dart. Managing these elements at the same time requires quite a lot of experience: the drape is something you check on the fitting bodice while it is open, whereas the armholes are corrected on a closed bodice.

THE BODICE

84

TRANSFERRING THE CORRECTIONS TO THE BASIC PATTERN

Transfer the corrections you have made on the muslin to the paper pattern, using a colored pencil so they are easy to see. Take out the pins to separate the back from the front. Also take out the pins that indicate the width of the darts.

Place the muslin back on the paper pattern back, first matching up the center back of the muslin with the center back drawn on the paper, then match up the horizontal construction lines: full hip line, waistline, armhole line, and upper chest line. Put a pin into each of their intersections with the center back line.

Before you go on to the next step, make sure that the muslin pattern is placed perfectly flat on top of the paper pattern, because the final result depends on this placement.

Now transfer the corrections that you made on the muslin to the paper pattern: The width of the back shoulder dart or the position of the waist darts, for example. Redraw the shoulder line or the shoulder slope as needed. All the marks that are indicated on the muslin should be transferred to the paper pattern. The muslin pattern and the paper pattern should be identical.

Note

Although you iron the muslin before cutting it, never iron it during the fitting. The heat and the steam can change the shape of the fabric.

Important

Pages 78 to 84 include explanations, advice, and demonstrations of corrective techniques for addressing the most common problems in the adjustment of the basic bodice. I recommend that you establish the corrections only on one side of the figure, left or right, then copy those corrections onto the other side, for instance by placing the muslin flat on a table.

It is well-known that the vertical (sagittal) symmetry of the body is not perfect. In most cases, the asymmetry is almost (or completely) invisible to the eye. But in cases where there are strong differences between the two sides, the adjustment of the basic pattern will have to be made by dealing with each side separately (one after the other). Make sure that the drape of the fabric indicated by the construction lines always remains perfectly vertical.

Whatever correction you are applying, you must never neglect the vertical drape of the center back and center front and the horizontal placement of the waistline.

FINISHED BASIC PATTERN

To be able to apply a variety of modifications to the basic pattern, depending on what designs you would like to create, you will have to remove the enlargements and the seam allowances, which could distort your result.

The widths for **basic enlargements** are rarely appropriate for all garments. In general, the width that you give to the garment depends on the clothing style, individual preferences, or level of comfort required. This is why it is desirable for the basic pattern not to include any enlargements. If there needs to be an enlargement, it is more appropriate to add it right before the basic pattern is manipulated to make it into a pattern for the desired design.

On the other hand, the **seam allowance** widths must be added to the finished pattern before applying any manipulations.

Establishing a basic pattern that includes the allowances requires you to have either memorized or written down, during the assembly and the muslin fitting, which edges have had seam allowances added and which have not. Thus, I advise you not to check your pattern with the seam allowances included, because that is hard to do right and often results in mistakes.

To avoid mistakes, once the basic pattern has been corrected during the fitting, copy it over (using tracing paper) without the enlargements or the seam allowances.

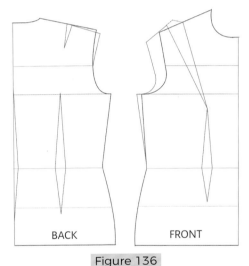

BACK   FRONT

Figure 136

TWO PATTERNS ON THE SAME DRAFT

Remember that a pattern is drafted in two main steps. The first involves establishing the global outline of the figure based on the given measurements (Figure 136, black lines). This pattern does not specify shapes. To adjust the pattern to the specific shape, transfer this basic structure onto the elements that will make it possible to emphasize the waist and to render the shapes of the bust, the hips, the rounding of the back, etc. visible. This adjustment can be obtained by applying darts (Figure 136, blue lines).

USING THE TWO PATTERNS

These two outlines cannot be separated from each other. You absolutely need a basic structure, the outline of the figure, to apply the darts to it.

The complete pattern (Figure 136), which includes the darts, is used for cutting the muslin and making the necessary adjustments to obtain a true imprint of the body. It is also used for most construction of fitted garments, such as jackets or sleeveless garments for which the presence of the front shoulder dart makes it possible to obtain an accurate armhole.

However, the pattern without darts is more appropriate for making things like a T-shirt, a wide tunic, or a garment cut out of a fabric that contains elastane. Thus, the choice of the pattern depends on the design.

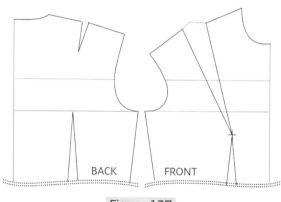

BACK   FRONT

Figure 137

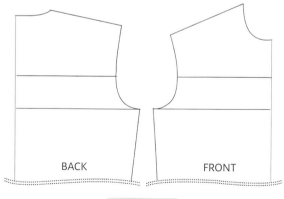

BACK   FRONT

Figure 138

EXAMPLES OF USE

To determine which pattern to use, you will first have to think about the design that you want to create and analyze its construction. First, locate the cut lines, then the width of the garment (for instance how full it is, whether the lines are close to the body or, on the other hand, extra wide). Then think about how low the armhole should go and the shape of the sleeve. Once this information is gathered, you can choose the pattern you need for the construction of the garment. Below, you can find a few examples of the use of one pattern or the other, depending on the design.

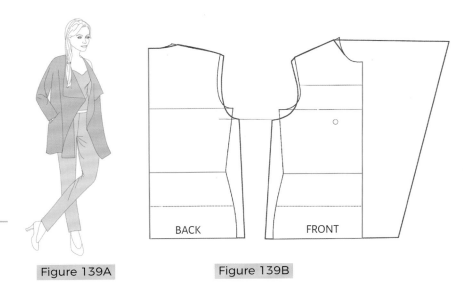

Figure 139A

Figure 139B

For this straight jacket design with a wide overlap and more of its shape falling toward the front, the manipulation (Figure 139B, in green) of the basic pattern (Figure 139B, in black) is established based on the simple pattern (without the darts).

The pattern for this lined jacket (Figure 140B, in green), whose bottom, sleeve, and collar finishings are made up of ribbing, is also based on the simple basic pattern (Figure 140B, in black).

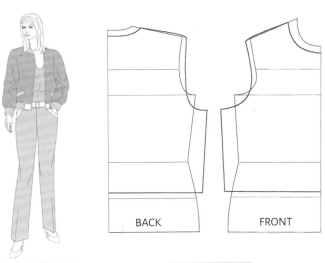

Figure 140A

Figure 140B

For this dress with kimono sleeves, which is wide at the waist and pulled together at the lower end by a broad sash, the choice leans, once again, toward a simple pattern without the basic darts.

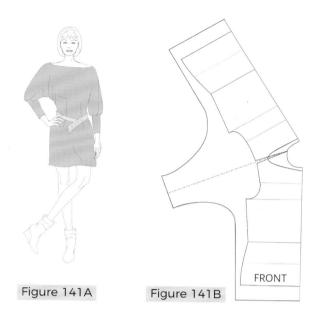

Figure 141A   Figure 141B

For this lightweight, unlined, closely fitted, button-up jacket with a classic princess seam, the cut lines of the design must be respected. The back shoulder darts and the front shoulder dart are shifted toward the armhole, then connected with the waist darts.

To manipulate the pattern to create this design, you will have to use the complete pattern, including the front shoulder darts, the back shoulder darts, and the waist darts.

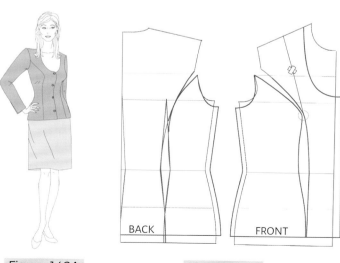

Figure 142A   Figure 142B

THE SLEEVE

In addition to the technical aspects, the sleeve's aesthetic dimension and comfort play an essential role. The shape and measurements of the sleeve cap, as well as the sleeve's height, width, and fullness, must correspond precisely with those of the armhole. The sleeve is unmistakably one of the most complex elements to construct and assemble, so take the time to read all of the explanations very carefully in order to understand the role of each line of the draft.

There is no basic pattern for sleeves. For every bodice, therefore, you will have to build a sleeve based on the armhole.

In this chapter, you will find all the necessary steps for a successful sleeve pattern. All you need is a little bit of patience!

IMPORTANT FEATURES
of the Sleeve

A sleeve that is comfortable and fits well is directly tied to two essential elements: the construction and the assembly. While in the construction of a bodice you base the work on measurements taken from the body, to which you may apply a few alterations to adjust the garment, it is very different for the sleeve.

This is because, in the construction of the sleeve, most measurements cannot be taken from the body (the length of the armhole, the height of the sleeve cap, the width of the sleeve, etc.), except, of course, for the measurements of the length and the contours. But even these are not used until checking the construction—not during the construction itself.

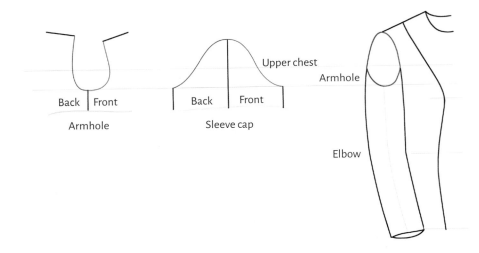

Armhole

Sleeve cap

Upper chest

Armhole

Elbow

The good draping and the comfort provided by an accurate assembly depend entirely on measurements taken from the armhole of the bodice, once it has been well-adjusted to the figure. As a result, the sleeve corresponds exclusively to the armhole of the bodice it was constructed for, and cannot, as a result, be used for any other garment.

Unlike the bodice, the skirt, or pants, for which there are basic patterns, there is no basic sleeve pattern—just like there is no basic neckline pattern. The sleeve must be constructed anew every time you change to a new design or style of garment.

NECESSARY MEASUREMENTS
for Sleeve Construction

As you just read on the previous page, the sleeve is constructed from the measurements taken from the bodice, adjusted to the shape, with the enlargements added in height and width (Figure 107, page 66). To make this happen, you will therefore need the following measurements: the depth of the armhole (in blue, Figure 143), the length of the back armhole (in red, Figure 143), the length of the front armhole (in green, Figure 143), and the width of the sleeve cap (Figure 145, page 94).

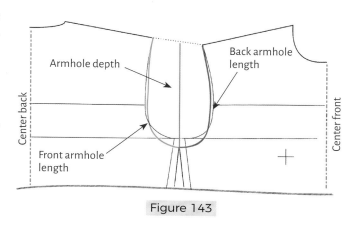

Figure 143

Armhole Depth

To obtain the depth of the armhole, place the back and the front side by side, matching up the horizontal lines of the upper chest and the armhole line, as in Figure 143. Connect the ends of the shoulders by drawing a straight line (black dotted line), then draw a vertical line (in blue, Figure 143) from the bottom of the armhole up to this straight line. Now measure the length of this vertical line: This is the depth of the armhole, which will allow you to calculate the height of the sleeve cap.

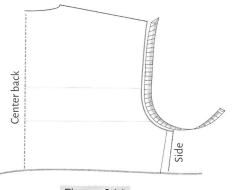

Figure 144

Back and Front Armhole Lengths

Using a tape measure, a flexible ruler, a string, or a piece of thread, make separate and accurate measurements of the lengths of the back armhole and the front armhole, meticulously following its shape. Write down these measurements, which will be used to determine the width of the sleeve, specific to the garment being made.

This measurement may possibly be corrected if it is different from the arm circumference (Figure 36, page 25).

Width of the Sleeve Cap

It often happens that arm movements are limited because the jacket or blouse is "pulling" and getting in the way of the arm moving forward. In this case, people often say that the back upper chest is not wide enough. But in fact, most often, it is not the width of the upper chest that creates this discomfort but rather the fact that the sleeve cap is too narrow.

This measurement is very important, because it is the proper width of the sleeve cap that allows the garment to be comfortable at the upper chest level.

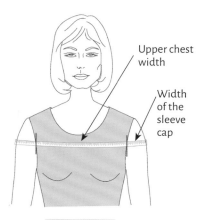

Figure 145

To calculate the width of the sleeve cap, subtract the back upper chest and front upper chest widths from the upper chest circumference measurement (Figure 145), and divide the result by two.

For example, the back upper chest width is 38 cm (Figure 19, page 19); the front upper chest width is 36 cm (Figure 22, page 20); the circumference of the body at that height is 118 cm. Thus, you have to subtract the width of the back upper chest (38 cm) and front upper chest (36 cm) from the total body circumference at the upper chest level (118 cm): 118 − (38 + 36) = 44 cm. The result (44 cm) corresponds to the total width of the two sleeve caps. If we divide this result by two (44 divided by 2), we get a width for each sleeve cap of 22 cm.

Using this measurement when you are constructing the sleeve ensures that the garment will be comfortable when it is made. Note that this measurement will be used when drafting the sleeve.

Calculating the Height of the Sleeve Cap

The height of the sleeve cap is very important in constructing the sleeve. If the sleeve cap is too large, too small, or the wrong shape for the armhole, it will throw off the vertical drape of the sleeve.

To get a measurement for the height of the sleeve cap that is properly adjusted to the armhole, subtract 1/5th of the measurement of the depth of the armhole.

For example, if the depth of the armhole is 22 cm (Figure 143, page 93), then 1/5th of 22 cm (22/5) is 4.4 cm. The height of the sleeve cap is thus 22 minus 4.4, or 17.6 cm.

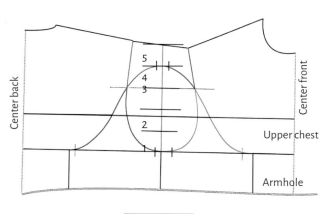

Figure 146

SLEEVE CONSTRUCTION

First of all, make sure that you have all of the measurements you need for constructing the sleeve:

- Armhole depth
- Back armhole length
- Front armhole length
- Sleeve cap width
- Neck depth
- Arm length
- Arm circumference

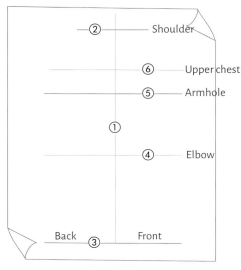

Figure 147

① In the middle of a piece of paper, about 50 x 70 cm, draw a long vertical line in red: this is the reference line that divides the sleeve into back and front parts; it also indicates the drape of the sleeve after the assembly.

② At the top of the paper, about 5 cm from the top, draw a horizontal line perfectly perpendicular to the red line: this is the shoulder line.

③ Draw another horizontal line at the bottom of the paper. The distance between this line and the shoulder line up top will be the total sleeve length.

④ Starting from the shoulder line, measure down the vertical line the distance of the shoulder-to-elbow length and draw a horizontal line at that point: this is the elbow line.

⑤ Again starting from the shoulder line, measure down the vertical line the distance of the height of the sleeve cap (Figure 146, page 94) and draw a horizontal line at that point: this is the armhole line.

⑥ From the armhole line, measure upward the distance calculated for the upper chest height. This is the same measurement that was calculated for the bodice (Figure 48, page 34).

95

Note

It is very important to double-check all the measurements and make sure that all of the lines you have drawn are both perfectly horizontal and perfectly perpendicular to the reference line (in red). The rest of the drawing and the final result depend on this first step of construction. A mistake at this stage would result in incorrect sleeve construction.

MEASUREMENTS OF THE SLEEVE CAP

A correctly constructed sleeve is one that perfectly follows the shape of the arched arm. For that to happen, the shape and size of the sleeve cap need to be perfectly matched to the armhole of the bodice.

You must put in the necessary time at this stage of the construction to achieve a comfortable garment that drapes well.

SLEEVE WIDTH

① The width of the sleeve is determined by the shape of the armhole and by the enlargements made to the bodice depending on the style of the garment. Therefore, every time you change the shape of the armhole and/or the enlargements, the width of the sleeve will also be modified in proportion.

To determine the width of the sleeve, you will use the back and front armhole lengths. Then you will calculate the width of the back of the sleeve (= 3/4 of the back armhole length) and the width of the front of the sleeve (= 3/4 of the front armhole length).

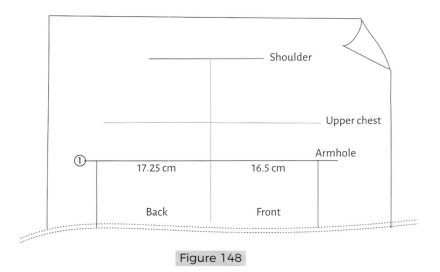

Figure 148

For example, back armhole length = 23 cm, front armhole length = 22 cm. The width of the sleeve in the back is 3/4 of 23 cm, or 17.25 cm; the width of the sleeve in the front is 3/4 of 22 cm, or 16.5 cm.

Once you have made these calculations, apply the results for the back and the front separately, along the armhole line in each case, and always starting at the reference line (in red, Figure 148). Then, at the width on either side, draw vertical lines down to the bottom of the sleeve.

② The measurement of the width of the upper chest (like the width of the sleeve) has to be balanced between the back part and the front part. To do this, calculate the difference between the back sleeve width and the front sleeve width.

For example, if we take the example from the previous page again: back sleeve width = 17.25 cm; front sleeve width = 16.5 cm; then the difference is 17.25 minus 16.5, or 0.75 cm.

If the width of the sleeve cap is 22 cm, then we take the difference we found above (0.75 cm) and add it to the back upper chest width and subtract it from the front upper chest width. Thus, the back upper chest width is 22/2 + 0.75, or 11.75 cm, and the front upper chest width is 22/2 minus 0.75, or 10.25 cm.

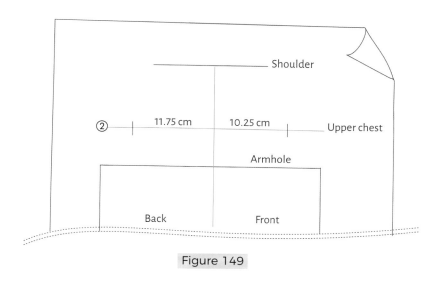

Figure 149

Following these examples, make the calculations on the pattern using the measurements you have taken. Then apply the results to the back and the front separately, in each case along the upper chest line and starting at the reference line (in red, Figure 149). Then, at the width, draw short verticals as shown in Figure 149.

97

FLAT AREAS AT THE SLEEVE CAP

The sleeve cap (like other elements that make up a garment) is made with flat areas. In general, these small flat spaces depend entirely on the shape of the figure (how full it is) and on the enlargements made to the garment (Figure 15, page 17).

For example, if the top has been enlarged by 3 cm, then the flat area on the curve at the sleeve cap that corresponds most closely should be 1.5 cm; if the top has been enlarged by 5 cm, that number is 2.5 cm.

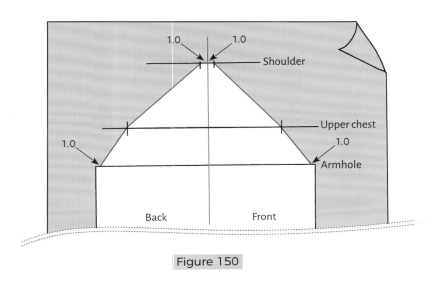

Figure 150

On the construction of the base pattern (which will be adjusted during the fitting), the planned enlargements are minimal to avoid opening up the armhole too much and carving out and flattening the head of the sleeve too much. Apply 1 cm of flat area to the end of the width of the sleeve cap (upper chest line, Figure 150), as well as 1 cm at the top of the sleeve cap, along the shoulder line, on either side of the red line (Figure 150). Then connect the points indicated in Figure 150 by straight lines, as shown in the figure.

SHAPE OF THE SLEEVE CAP

There are as many ways to obtain a shape for the sleeve cap that perfectly matches the armhole as there are pattern makers. Every pattern maker has their own technique for obtaining the best result.

The method presented here is the simplest possible, in terms of both the approach and the implementation. To draw the rounded shape of the sleeve cap, work from several different reference points. Because the marks placed at the width and the flat areas are not enough, you will have to add additional reference marks.

Divide the upper part of the sleeve cap (from the shoulder line to the upper chest line, blue lines, Figure 151) by 2, and at the halfway mark draw short perpendicular lines (Figure 151), 1.8 cm long in the back and 1.5 cm long in the front.

Now divide the lower part of the sleeve cap (from the upper chest line to the armhole line, green lines, Figure 151) by 3. One third of the distance up from the armhole line (or 2/3 of the distance down from the upper chest line), draw short perpendicular lines, 0.5 cm long in the back and 0.8 cm long in the front.

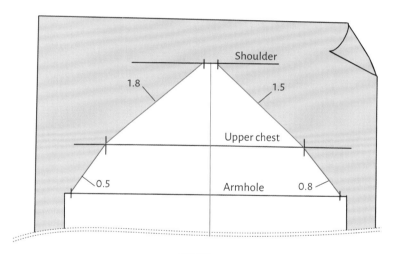

Figure 151

99

Note

The values assigned to the reference marks are approximate. They can be increased or decreased as needed during the checking of the measurements (see page 102).

DRAFTING THE SLEEVE CAP

To draw the shape of the sleeve cap correctly, use a curved tool: The French curve ruler. The one shown here, with its variety of curves, is easily adaptable to the desired shapes.

To draw the shapes of the sleeve cap, several different steps are required. Start the drawing at the top. Find a curve on the French curve ruler that can connect the points of the flat area along the shoulder line, the reference point, and the width of the back upper chest.

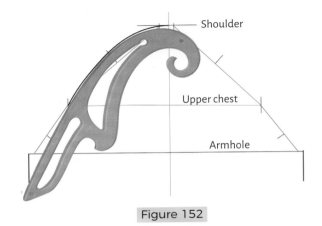

Figure 152

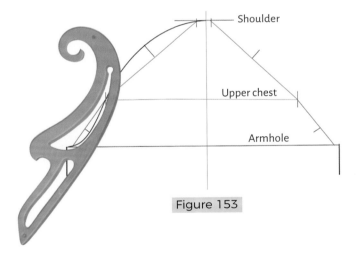

Figure 153

To finish the shape of the back sleeve cap, turn the French curve around and connect the point marking the upper chest width to the flat area of the sleeve width. It is important for the whole curve, and in particular the connection between the two segments of the curve, to be continuous, without jags, depressions, or bulges (see the sleeve in Figure 156).

Note

The positions of the French curve shown here for drawing the shape of the sleeve cap are given as an example. While these positions are the best suited for the configurations illustrated here, they can change depending on the outline of the sleeve (the height of the sleeve cap or the upper chest line, the width of the sleeve at the armhole or the upper chest). The position of the French curve should be adjusted in such a way that the chosen curve can connect the various reference points.

In the same way as the back, draw the shape of the front of the sleeve. Start at the sleeve cap, respecting the flat area (Figure 154). Then draw the bottom of the sleeve: From the upper chest line to the armhole line, position the French curve in such a way that its shape corresponds to the reference marks on the sleeve (Figure 155).

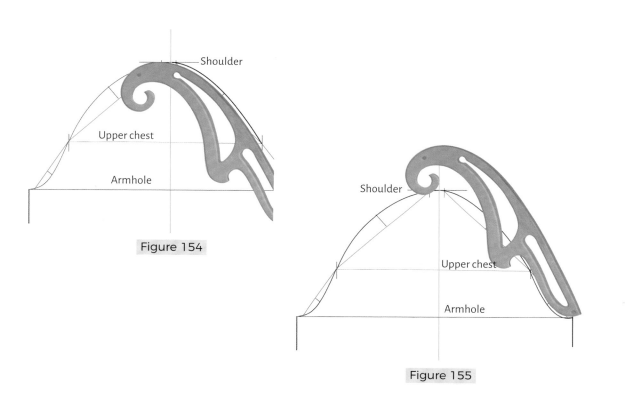

Figure 154

Figure 155

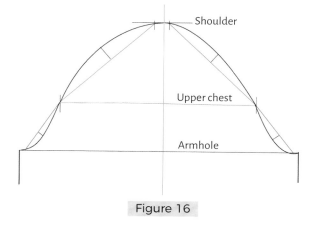

Figure 16

The shape of the sleeve cap, drawn like this from approximate reference points, is not definitive.

The length of the edge of the sleeve cap must absolutely correspond to the length of the armhole, and thus you will have to check this correspondence and, if necessary, correct it by increasing or decreasing the length of the edges of the sleeve cap.

CHECKING SLEEVE CAP AND ARMHOLE MEASUREMENTS

Before anything else, you must check the measurements of the length of the sleeve cap: do they match up correctly with the measurements of the armhole, in such a way that during assembly, the sleeve can easily enter into and be assembled with the armhole?

Note that the seam allowance for this assembly is always pressed toward the sleeve, thus the sleeve cap will need to have enough give to surround the armhole.

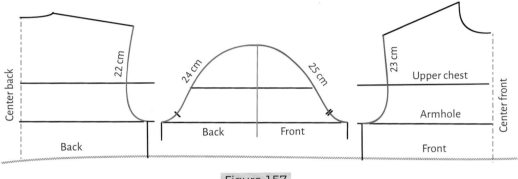

Figure 157

This bit of extra given to the sleeve cap is the sleeve cap margin. It depends on the style of the garment (jacket with or without shoulder pads, for example) and the thickness and quality of the fabric: a flexible fabric will be easier to absorb during assembly than a rigid one. The minimum margin to be added to the length of the sleeve cap edge is 2 cm (Figure 158).

The length measurements are taken using a tape measure or a flexible ruler. This stage of construction is important because it allows you to determine the corrections that you will have to make next.

When you increase or decrease the measurements of the sleeve cap length, make sure to respect the height of the sleeve cap, the width of the upper chest line, and the flat areas of the armhole and the shoulder line; these elements must not be modified.

The measurements are adjusted by moving the curved lines (black, green, and red lines on Figure 158), changing the values of the reference marks that were placed during the construction of the sleeve cap (Figure 151, page 99).

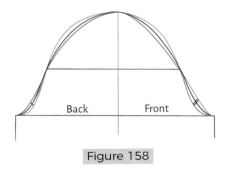

Figure 158

DISTRIBUTING THE MARGIN AROUND THE SLEEVE CAP

The minimum measurement for the margin to be added around the sleeve cap is 2 cm. This is what you will use when you are constructing the basic pattern.

For example, if the length of the back armhole is 22 cm, the length of the back sleeve cap needs to be 24 cm (blue lines, Figure 157). Similarly, for the front: if the front armhole length is 23 cm (green line, Figure 157), the front sleeve cap length needs to be 25 cm.

The 2 cm of margin added to the back length and the 2 cm added to the front length of the sleeve cap must be proportionally distributed between the lower and upper part: 1 cm between the upper chest and armhole of the sleeve and 1 cm between the upper chest and shoulder line (Figure 159).

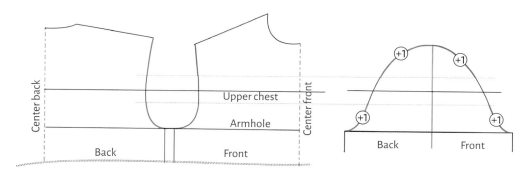

Figure 159

The short straight line (in black, Figure 159), approximately 4 cm long (2 cm below and 2 cm above the upper chest line), indicates the part of the sleeve cap that does not absorb any of the margin. During the assembly of the sleeve, there should be no surplus at that spot. The two layers of fabric (the armhole and the sleeve) are assembled flat.

Note

The width of the margin from the armhole to the upper chest line is 1 cm, in general, but it can vary depending on the thickness of the fabric.

If this measurement is too large, the lower part of the sleeve will balloon, because there is too much fabric to absorb, producing a wrinkled or gathered effect.

If the margin is 3 cm wide, as is the case for a suit-jacket sleeve, for example, you will assign 1 cm to the lower part of the sleeve (from armhole to upper chest line) and 2 cm to the upper part (upper chest line to shoulder).

ASSEMBLY NOTCHES

Correctly assembling the sleeve and the armhole together is not easy, especially because the distribution of the sleeve cap margin all around the length of the armhole is somewhat problematic.

 To make this assembly easier and to guide the process, you will need to place assembly notches along the sleeve back, front, and cap.

> ## Note
>
> The numbers shown in Figure 160 are given as an example to illustrate the points made here. They can change depending on the width of the sleeve at the level of the armhole line, the height of the sleeve cap, and the width of the sleeve at the upper chest line.

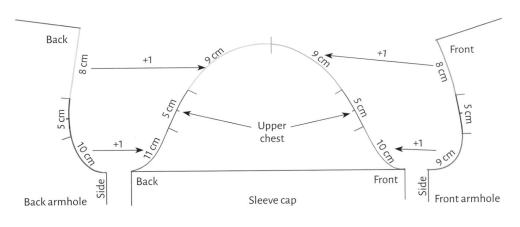

Figure 160

Place the first notch on the back armhole, at the spot where the curved shape of the armhole underneath the arm is the straightest (in green, Figure 160).

 Then, using a flexible ruler or a tape measure, measure the distance from this notch to the side line.

 Add 1 cm to this measurement and transfer it to the sleeve cap (in green).

 Starting at the first notch placed on the armhole, measure 4 to 5 cm (distance shown in black, Figure 160), and draw the next notch. In the same way as before, place the notch on the edge of the sleeve cap. This part will be assembled flat and will not absorb any of the margin—it corresponds to the upper chest level on the body.

The third part of the sleeve, which goes to the notch placed at the top of the sleeve cap (in yellow on the back, Figure 160), includes 1 cm of margin, which will be absorbed by the armhole.

To place the assembly notches on the front part of the sleeve and the armhole, proceed in the same way as for the back.

If the distribution of the assembly notches matches with the sleeve length and armhole measurements, proceed to the next stage of construction. If not, revisit the lengths (Figure 157, page 102). Don't forget to place the reference notches on the sleeve cap (see page 17).

SLEEVE DART

In addition to an accurate drape based on good construction and assembly, the sleeve needs to have an arched shape—necessary both for the sake of aesthetics and to allow the arm to move comfortably.

This is made possible by using a dart at the level of the elbow. On the basic construction of the sleeve, this dart is placed along the horizontal line of the elbow, but like all darts, it can be moved.

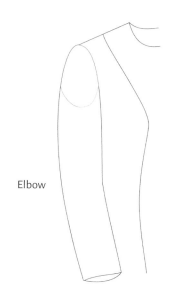

Elbow

CONSTRUCTING THE DART

To continue drafting the sleeve, draw vertical lines at the width of the sleeve determined at the armhole line (Figure 148, page 96) to the line that establishes its length (Figure 143, page 93).

At this stage of the construction, the drawing represents a straight, rather wide sleeve. To give it a narrower shape, you will have to reduce its width toward the end, and to ensure that it is comfortable to wear, you will need to apply the dart at the elbow.

To avoid throwing off the drape of the sleeve, determine the desired width of its lower end (in blue, Figure 161), by subtracting (from the total width of the bottom of the sleeve) the same length on either side, starting at the two ends of the bottom of the sleeve (black portions of the lines along the bottom of the sleeve, Figure 161).

For example, the total width of the bottom of the sleeve = 33 cm (this is the width of the sleeve determined along the armhole line, then transferred to the line of the base of the sleeve). The desired width of the bottom of the sleeve = 22 cm. The difference between these two widths (33 minus 22) = 11 cm. This difference must then be divided by two: 11/2 = 5.5 cm. This gives us the distance to be subtracted from either side, at each extremity of the width of the bottom of the sleeve.

Apply these calculations, as explained above, then draw straight lines starting from the armhole all the way down to the bottom of the sleeve (green lines, Figure 161).

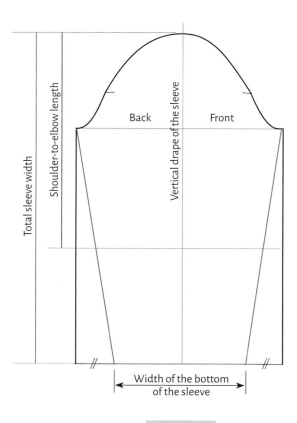

Figure 161

REFERENCE POINTS FOR THE SLEEVE DART

To be able to draw the sleeve dart on the pattern, you will have to locate several elements, of which one of the most important is the position of the elbow.

① To do this, divide the width of the sleeve back by two and draw a vertical line to the elbow line. The intersection of these two lines corresponds to the elbow (red cross, Figure 162).

② At the level of the elbow line, extend the line of the width of the sleeve back by 1.5 cm toward the outside of the drawing and make a mark. Then subtract the same amount along the line of the width of the sleeve front (toward the inside of the drawing) and make another mark. These reference points will be used to tilt the lower part of the sleeve forward, following the arched shape of the arm. Each of the following steps will allow you to capture the necessary modification of the drawing better and better.

③ Draw short horizontal lines (dotted lines, Figure 162) 2 cm above and 2 cm below the elbow line, and on the two sides of the width of the sleeve (back side and front side). These reference lines will allow you to position the flat areas along the curved lines of the sleeve.

④ Starting from the edge of the bottom of the back sleeve, draw a vertical line 3 cm long. The width of the dart will then be recuperated at the bottom of the sleeve, thanks to this reference mark.

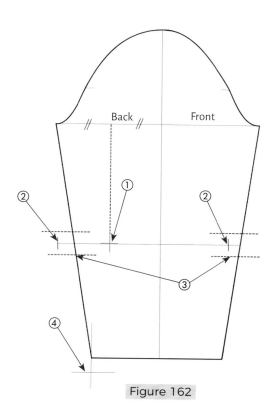

Figure 162

LENGTH OF THE FRONT OF THE SLEEVE

Before putting in the elbow dart, you are going to determine the shape of the sleeve. You will redraw the sleeve's final lines using the reference marks that you placed previously.

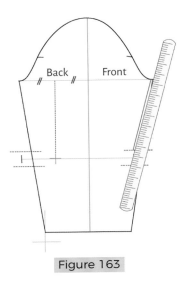

Figure 163

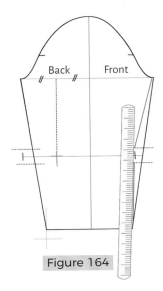

Figure 164

Using a ruler, join the end of the front armhole with the reference mark placed on the elbow line; but only draw the corresponding straight line as far as the dotted line to maintain the flat area of the elbow (Figure 163).

Proceed in the same way for the lower part of the sleeve: connect the front extremity of the width of the bottom of the sleeve with the reference mark placed along the elbow line, but only draw the straight line as far as the dotted line to maintain the flat area of the elbow (Figure 164).

Finally, draw the section between these two straight lines, which corresponds to the flat area of the elbow (Figure 165), using a French curve. This line must be continuous and gently curved (in green, Figure 166).

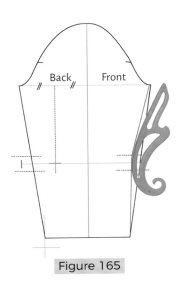

Figure 165

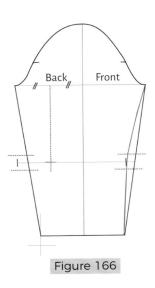

Figure 166

The back part of the sleeve is drafted the same way as the front part, using a ruler and a French curve.

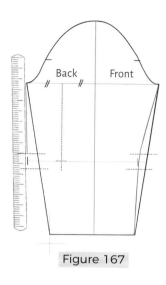

Figure 167

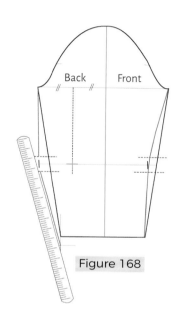

Figure 168

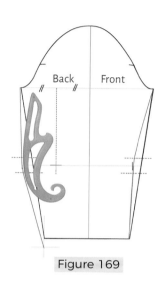

Figure 169

Draw a straight line connecting the back of the armhole at the reference point along the elbow line, only as far as the flat area (Figure 167). Then, at the point that extends the line of the bottom of the sleeve (4, Figure 162, page 107), draw a straight line connecting the reference point to the flat area (Figure 168). Finally, connect these two lines with a light curve, using a French curve ruler (Figure 169).

PLACING THE ELBOW DART

The elbow dart is about 3 cm wide—it is hardly ever more than that, and even less often less than that. Consider the elbow line (black line, Figure 170) as the axis of this dart and measure 1.5 cm on either side of it. Connect the elbow point with the straight lines (in blue, Figure 170). Now you have positioned the dart.

Closing this dart will slightly change the shape of the line of the back of the sleeve, so you will have to redraw that line.

Figure 170

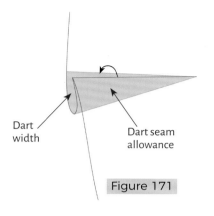

Fold the dart by laying the lower sleeve on top of the upper sleeve, with the width of the dart pressed toward the back (Figure 171). Then, using a French curve, redraw the line. A small dart "cap" will appear. Its shape depends on the slope of the line, in other words, the width of the bottom of the sleeve.

Dart width

Dart seam allowance

Figure 171

RESTORING THE BOTTOM OF THE SLEEVE

Inserting the dart at the elbow changes the line of the bottom of the sleeve. To draw the new line of the bottom of the sleeve, start by establishing the right angles (90 degrees) of the edges of the sleeve. Otherwise, after the sleeve is assembled, the line along its lower end will not be straight.

Place a ruler on the line of the length of the back of the sleeve and draw a short perpendicular line (2 to 3 cm) starting at the lower end of the sleeve (in blue, Figure 172). Do the same for the front of the sleeve (in blue, Figure 173).

Then, using a French curve (Figure 174), connect these short lines that you have just drawn (which indicate the edges of the sleeve). This line should be continuous and almost straight.

Note

On the outline of the pattern, if the slope of a vertical or horizontal line has been changed, the right angles will also have to be checked and, if necessary, restored, so as not to create hollows or "beaks" after the two edges of the piece have been assembled.

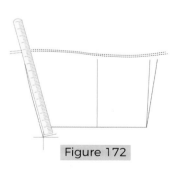

Figure 172

Figure 173

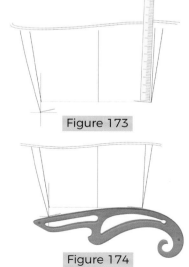

Figure 174

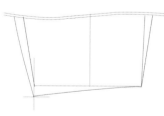

Figure 175

FINISHED SLEEVE PATTERN

You have now completed drafting the sleeve for the basic bodice.

The finished pattern must include the necessary indications for proper assembly. Before placing the pattern on the fabric and cutting it out, add the 1 cm seam allowance and check very carefully whether all reference notches (page 17)—on the back and front of the sleeve—and assembly notches are present and correctly placed. On the sleeve, the drape (red vertical line on the pattern) corresponds to the straight grain of the fabric.

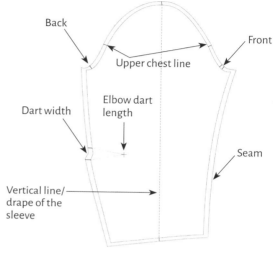

Back

Front

Upper chest line

Elbow dart length

Dart width

Seam

Vertical line/ drape of the sleeve

Figure 176

CUTTING INTO
the Muslin Fabric

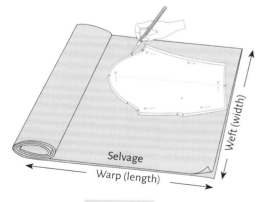

Selvage

Warp (length)

Weft (width)

Figure 177

Place the sleeve pattern on a double thickness of fabric, paying attention to the straight grain. Pin the pattern and the fabric together at several points and then trace the outline onto the fabric. The length of the elbow dart is drawn on the muslin in the same way as the waist darts (Figures 91 and 92, page 60).

Now remove the paper pattern and put a few pins inside the outline of the sleeve, keeping the two layers of fabric together—this means that you will be cutting two pieces (left and right) that are perfectly identical.

Notch the edges by about 0.5 cm at the places indicated by the assembly and reference notches.

ASSEMBLY
- - - - - - -
SLEEVE ASSEMBLY

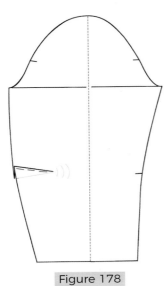

Figure 178

The fitting sleeve for the basic bodice has little enlargement, aside from the necessary width for adjusting the sleeve.

To be perfectly safe during the fitting, in other words to avoid having the person be poked by the pins (especially under their arms!), you will have to assemble the sleeves using a basting stitch (a temporary hand stitch using a double thread).

Close the elbow dart by pressing its width toward the back and then basting it closed (in green, Figure 178).

Now close up the sleeve along its length. For this assembly seam not to produce extra thickness, and so that it will be flat without having to be ironed, lay the two seam allowances on top of each other and assemble them. To make this assembly easier, place a fairly wide, long ruler inside the sleeve (Figure 179).

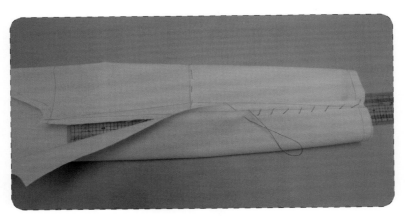

Figure 179

ASSEMBLING SLEEVE AND ARMHOLE TOGETHER

As already noted at the beginning of this chapter, the drafting and assembly of the sleeve involve rather delicate work, requiring a lot of precision. Here is a brief reminder of the rules of assembly.

The armhole curve (in blue, Figure 180) has to accommodate and absorb the 1 cm surplus of the sleeve cap.

At about 2 cm above and 2 cm below the upper chest line, the edges of the armhole and of the sleeve cap should be assembled flat (without any excess fabric margin). Finally, the sleeve cap includes 1 cm of margin that must be absorbed by the armhole (in green, Figure 180).

There are several methods for correctly assembling the sleeve with the armhole.

What makes this assembly particularly demanding is the extra fabric of the margin along the sleeve cap, which must be regularly distributed without creating folds. You can, for example, apply a double seam to the edge of the sleeve cap, then create a gather by pulling the threads; or you can pin all around the armhole every half centimeter...or use any other technique that is more or less efficient, fast, or easy to grasp. Every method is a good method as long as it produces an accurate drape and a nice-looking visual effect for the sleeve.

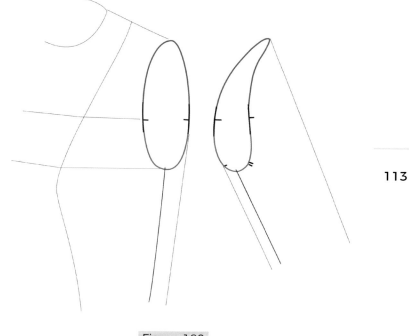

Figure 180

In the following pages, you will find a relatively easy and fast assembly method. Even though it is somewhat complex, you can manage it successfully on the first try if you follow the explanations given here very carefully. You must therefore take the time necessary to carry out this assembly without rushing or skipping any of the steps.

ASSEMBLY STEPS

Start by positioning the sleeve cap inside the armhole and secure it in place with a few pins. The actual assembly must be carried out with a basting stitch (preferably by hand) and not using pins (which run the risk of hurting the person being fitted).

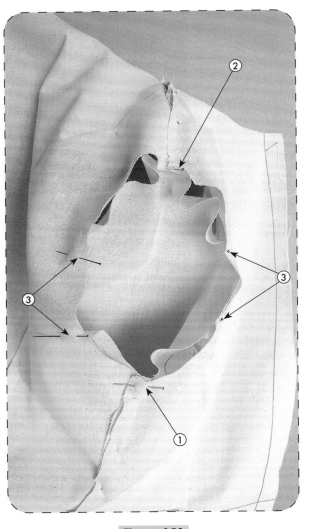

Figure 181

① Place the sleeve inside the armhole in such a way that the piece is inside out (Figure 181). In other words, we are pinning the outside to the outside. Match up the seams of the bottom of the armhole and of the sleeve cap; place a pin there.

② Now align the notch placed at the top of the sleeve with the shoulder seam; place a pin there.

③ Match up, face to face, the two notches that indicate the upper chest heights (of the armhole and of the sleeve cap), flatten the edges, then pin about 2 cm above the notch and 2 cm below it.

Double your thread so that the assembly seam is solid and start basting the bottom of the armhole to the edge of the sleeve cap, maintaining the seam allowance.

In the armhole curve, there is 1 cm that has to be absorbed: lightly pull the two edges (of the armhole and the sleeve cap) between the pins. Because they are cut along a curve, they stretch easily. And, because the distances are small at this point, you can perfectly well hold the two layers of fabric in position in your fingers while sewing a fairly tight basting stitch (about every 3 mm).

The part from the upper chest to the top of the sleeve cap, on the other hand, is not as easy to sew, because the edge of the armhole does not stretch easily there. To distribute the sleeve cap surplus evenly, you will have to do your basting by passing through the fabric with a needle every 4 to 5 millimeters.

Figure 182

FITTING AND CORRECTIONS

The first thing you need to check on the sleeve, once it is assembled, is how the seams of the sleeve and the side of the bodice match up. The two lines should be nicely aligned from the armhole down to the waist. Place the piece on a mannequin or on a table and fold the sleeve above the elbow (Figure 183).

If the two seams are properly aligned, then proceed to the next step. If they are not, there are two possible causes: a construction mistake or, less often, an assembly mistake. Either way, a mistake has been made at some point.

If that happens, go back to the pattern and check the widths allocated to the back and the front of the sleeve at the armhole line (Figure 148, page 96), and then check the width given to the bottom of the sleeve (Figure 161, page 106) and make the necessary corrections depending on the step at which you made the mistake.

If the construction is fine, then it may be a mistake in absorbing the sleeve cap surplus during assembly that you will have to review.

Figure 183

DRAPE OF THE SLEEVE

The most important thing in making a garment is the drape of the fabric. This is what both makes it comfortable and provides a successful aesthetic effect. The drape can be easily thrown off by a mistake in construction (failing to maintain the parallel and perpendicular lines) or by an assembly error (failing to match up the notches correctly).

Put the basic bodice on the model and close up the front with a few pins, making sure to connect the horizontal construction lines drawn on both sides (left and right) (Figures 131 and 132, page 82).

As with the center front and back of the bodice, the drape line of the sleeve must be nice and vertical. It must absolutely start at the shoulder seam (Figure 184) and fall perfectly parallel to the side line (Figure 185).

In general, the upper chest and armhole lines should correspond to the same lines on the bodice, after the piece is assembled. A small discrepancy of about 1 to 2 cm between the two upper chest lines (on the bodice and on the sleeve) can however be tolerated. The two armhole lines, on the other hand, must absolutely be at the same level.

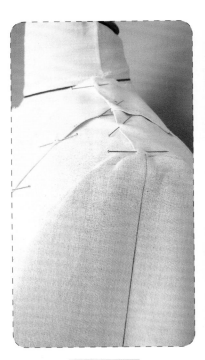

Figure 184

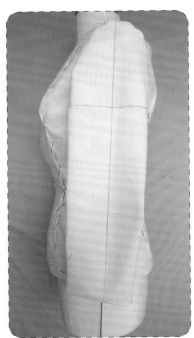

Figure 185

MOST COMMON PROBLEM

A well-constructed sleeve cap should be able to be overlaid with the armhole without producing any creases or distortions (Figure 186). The surplus of the upper part of the sleeve cap must cover the seam allowance of the armhole. If any part of the sleeve (in front or in back) detaches itself from the bodice, or if it does not match up well with the armhole and creases appear (Figure 187), either the sleeve cap margin was not well distributed (because the notches were placed incorrectly, for example; Figure 160, page 104) or there was not enough surplus given to the sleeve cap between the armhole and the upper chest (Figure 157, page 102). In that case, you have to increase it. In most cases, when you encounter this problem it is with body shapes where the shoulder curve or arm circumference is rounded and full.

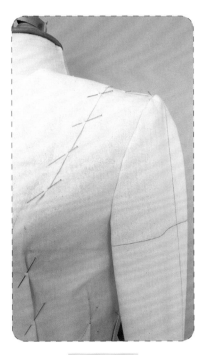

Figure 186

Figure 10

Note

The seam allowance for the assembly seam connecting the sleeve with the armhole is pressed toward the sleeve.

THE SKIRT

The construction of a basic skirt is not as complicated as that of a bodice because its outline is within the vertical extension of the bodice, from the full hip line downward. Nevertheless, because the skirt has to hold up at the waist, it is necessary to apply certain modifications to the waistline by playing with the darts and respecting the vertical drape of the fabric.

This is why you must absolutely not succumb to the temptation of using a bodice pattern as the basis for a skirt pattern. The basic skirt pattern must be drafted and adjusted to the body shape independently of the bodice.

Before You Start

Prepare the necessary measurements for drafting the skirt (see page 26): bust point to bust point, waist circumference, and full hip circumference.

The basic skirt pattern is always drawn starting at the waist. The length of the basic skirt stops at the knees, at a length of about 55 to 60 cm, depending on the person's height.

During the fitting, it is hard to judge the correct drape for a longer skirt: the vertical line can be thrown off by the shape of the legs. The desired length will be established when the basic pattern is transformed into a finished pattern (see pages 183 to 185).

Starting from the full hip line, the outline is vertical down to the knees.

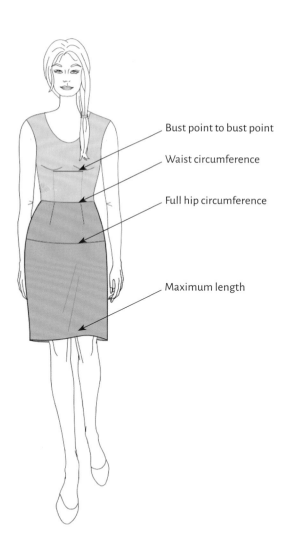

Bust point to bust point

Waist circumference

Full hip circumference

Maximum length

DRAFTING THE PATTERN

The straight skirt pattern is made up of two parts: the half-back and the half-front (see page 15).

It doesn't matter whether you start drafting the pattern in the front or in the back, unlike with the construction of the bodice, where the calculations made on the back are then transferred to the front.

The only difference between the back and the front of the skirt is their width, but you can draw either one of them first without it making any difference.

In drafting the basic straight skirt presented below, you will start with the back.

DRAFTING THE BACK

Take a sheet of about 60 x 100 cm and position it horizontally.

① On the left side of the sheet, about 3 to 5 cm from the edge, draw a red vertical line (red because this is a reference line), about 55 to 60 cm long: this is the center back line.

② At the top of the sheet, about 3 to 5 cm from the edge, draw a horizontal line, also in red: this is the second reference line, the waistline.

③ At the bottom of the center back line, draw a line perpendicular to that one: this horizontal line is the bottom of the skirt.

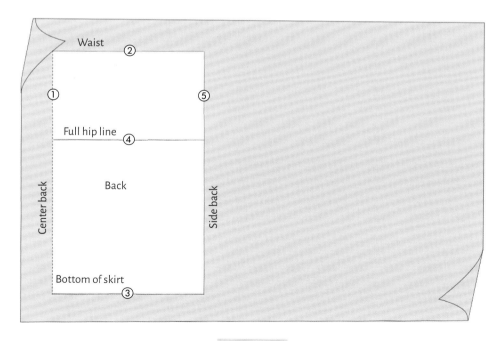

Figure 188

④ Starting from the waistline: Along the center back line, transfer the measurement of the full hip length (Figure 32, page 23) and draw a horizontal line at that point; this is the full hip line.

⑤ To close up the frame of the half-back, transfer the measurement of 1/4 of the full hip circumference, minus 1 cm, starting from the center back line along the waistline—in order to position the side line, see Figures 13 and 14, page 16. Starting from the end of this line, draw a vertical line down to the bottom of the skirt: this is the side back line.

A Good Thing to Know

Some methods recommend drawing the back and the front of the basic skirt pattern starting from the same side line—see Figure 189.

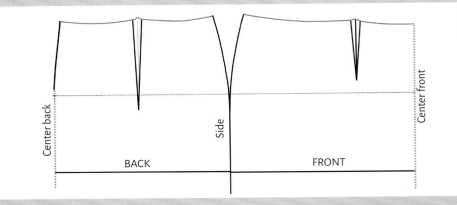

Figure 189

Without saying anything against these methods, I will just say that it is important to remember the purpose of drafting the basic pattern. It will be used either to apply the manipulations needed to obtain the desired design, or else as a basis for the adjustments to the particular body shape made during the fitting. In either case, then, it will be necessary at some point in time to separate the back from the front. If the back and the front are drawn starting along the same side line, each of the lines will then have to be traced over, adding another step to the work.

I strongly advise you to draft the back and the front separately on your sheet, leaving enough room between the two so that you can apply any modifications necessary as well as the seam allowances and enlargement allowances without having to copy over the original draft.

DRAFTING THE FRONT

At about 5 cm from the back side line, draw a parallel line: this is the front side line. Then, starting from this line, extend all of the horizontal lines: the waist (in red), the full hip line, and the bottom of the skirt. In order to draw the center front line, transfer the measurement of 1/4 of the full hip circumference, plus 1 cm, starting from the waistline. Starting from the end of this measurement, draw a vertical line to the bottom of the skirt: this is the center front line, and it is in red, because it is a reference line.

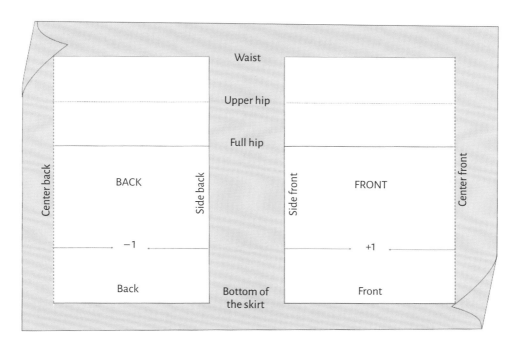

Figure 190

Note

Before going on to the next stage of construction, make sure that the measurements have been correctly applied and that the vertical and horizontal construction lines are accurately placed.

WAIST DARTS

POSITIONING THE WAIST DARTS

You will need to follow the order given here for positioning the darts; this is an important step for obtaining the right result.

① The first dart is placed at the bust-point-to-bust-point measurement. It is 9 cm long.

② The next dart is first placed on the front side, then at the same place on the back side. Its length depends on the body shape, but it generally stops around the level of the upper hips.

③ The skirt has a center back dart. The construction of this dart on the skirt is obligatory, unlike on the bodice, where it can be optional. On the basic pattern, this dart is 1 cm wide, but it can be increased during the fitting if the person's body shape makes that necessary.

④ The main dart of the half-back is placed halfway between the side back dart and the center back dart. The axis of the dart is thus drawn halfway between the two. It is 11 cm long.

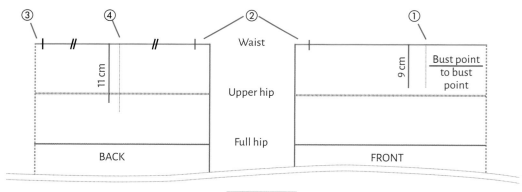

Figure 191

WAIST DART WIDTHS

For the fabric to adjust nicely to the shape of the figure, you need to reduce the excess fabric at the waist. And in order not to throw off the drape of the fabric, you will need to distribute the widths of the darts evenly around the waist. In other words, you need to absorb the same amount of fabric on each panel of the skirt (the two half-fronts and the two half-backs).

First of all, you need to know the difference between the waist circumference and the full hip circumference, then divide that number by 4 (see pages 56 and 57, "Calculating the waist dart widths").

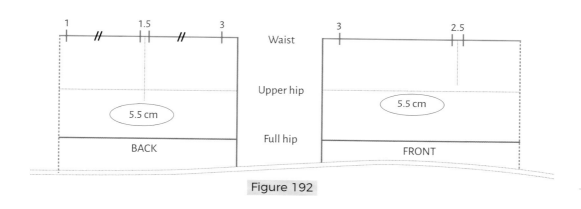

Figure 192

125

For example, the full hip circumference (92) minus the waist circumference (70) is 22. 22 divided by 4 = 5.5 cm.

The total width to be absorbed at the waist is 22 cm (the difference between the full hip circumference, 92 cm, and the waist circumference, 70 cm). Thus, it is necessary to absorb 5.5 cm on each panel of the skirt (Figure 192).

In the example shown here, this means that you need to create a 5.5-cm-wide dart on each of the two panels of the basic straight skirt pattern, making sure not to exceed the maximum width for each dart (Figure 83, page 55).

Here is the distribution of the darts for the example shown in Figure 192 and, as a reminder, in parentheses, the maximum widths for each dart:

- Bust-point-to-bust-point dart: 2.5 cm (max: 3 cm)
- Side darts: 3 cm (max: 4 cm)
- Middle of half-back dart: 1.5 cm (max: 2 cm)
- Center back dart: 1 cm (max: 1 cm)

ADDITIONAL DARTS

In the example shown in Figure 192, page 125, the width of the darts drafted on each panel does not exceed the maximum values, but if the difference between the measurements of the full hip and the waist is very large, you will have to insert additional darts.

For example, the full hip circumference is 94 and the waist circumference is 68. 94 minus 68 = 26, so there are 26 cm to be absorbed.

26/4 = 6.5 cm, so there are 6.5 cm to be absorbed on each of the panels, in other words 6.5 cm on each half-back and each half-front.

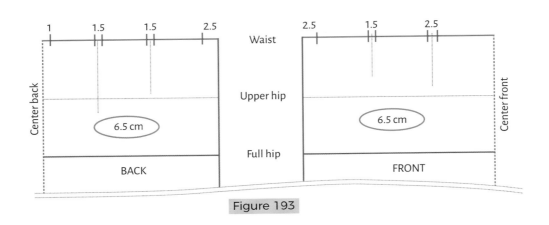

Figure 193

Additional Dart Widths

First, define the width of each dart.

In the case presented above, on the **front**, the main bust point dart = 2.5 cm; the side dart = 2.5 cm; and the additional dart = 1.5 cm. Total for all the darts = 6.5 cm.

The **back** includes the center back dart = 1 cm; the main dart in the middle of the half-back = 1.5 cm; the additional dart = 1.5 cm; and the side dart = 2.5 cm. Total for all the darts = 6.5 cm.

Placement of the Additional Darts

Front

The first dart is placed starting at the center front and following the bust-point-to-bust-point measurement. Draw the axis of this dart, making it 9 cm long. Then mark the width of the dart (2.5 cm), distributing it equally on either side of the axis (1.25 cm on each side).

The second dart is placed on the side of the skirt. Indicate its width by measuring 2.5 cm starting from the side line (in blue on Figure 194).

The third (additional) dart is placed halfway between the arm of the main (bust point to bust point) dart and the arm of the side dart. Measure the distance between these two dart arms (Figure 194), divide the distance by two, and then draw a vertical line (the axis of the additional dart) at that measurement. Then indicate the width of that dart (1.5 cm), distributed equally on either side of the axis (0.75 cm on each side). The additional darts are 2 to 3 cm shorter than the main darts (Figure 88, page 58).

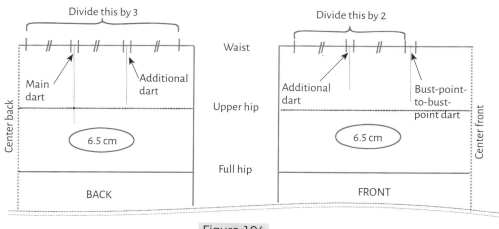

Figure 194

127

Back

First place the marks indicating the widths of the center back (1 cm) and side (2.5 cm) darts. Then measure the distance between the arms of these two darts. Divide this distance into three equal parts and draw the vertical lines, which are the axes of the darts.

The main dart has an axis length of 11 cm. In general, the additional dart is 2 to 3 cm shorter than the main dart (depending on the body shape). Indicate the width of this dart (1.5 cm) distributed evenly on either side of the axis (0.75 cm on each side).

DRAFTING THE DART SHAPES

Using a ruler, draw the arms of the darts (the bust-point-to-bust-point dart, Figure 195, and the dart at the middle of the half-back, Figure 196), connecting the point indicating the bottom of the dart with the reference points marking the width of the darts on either side of the axis, along the waistline.

The line of the front side dart is slightly rounded at the level of the upper hip line. To achieve this shape, use a French curve, placing it as shown in Figure 195. Then, to achieve the same shape for the back side dart, make marks on the French curve at the level of the waist and of the upper hips (in red on Figure 195). Then turn the French curve around and match the marks up with the corresponding line. Now draw the line on the side back, maintaining the width of the dart.

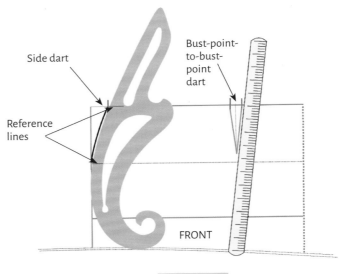

Figure 195

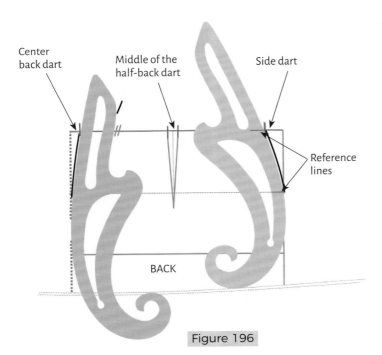

Figure 196

Draw the center back dart with an almost-straight line. But in order not to have a sharp point where the two lines meet, use the straight side of the French curve, as shown in Figure 196.

WAISTLINES

FRONT WAISTLINE

Once the darts are closed, the straight line of the waist that was drawn on the pattern will no longer be straight. To adjust it, and adapt it to the shape of the body, lower the waist along the middle line by 1.5 cm (Figure 197). Close the dart by pressing its width toward the center and keep it in this position using a pin.

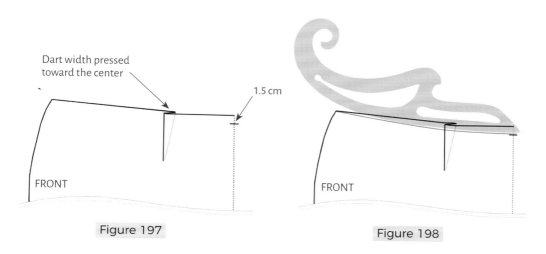

Figure 197

Figure 198

Using a French curve positioned as in Figure 198, redraw the waistline. Make sure that the intersection of the waistline with the center front line forms a neat right angle (Figure 199), so that there isn't either a hollow or a "beak" in the center, because the pattern will be cut on fold.

For the same reason, the waistline and the front side line must be perfectly perpendicular (Figure 199) so that you have a smooth, straight line once you have assembled the back and front together.

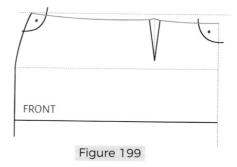

Figure 199

Note

If the construction includes several darts placed at the waist on the half-back or half-front, all of the darts need to be closed and then kept closed with pins before restoring the waistline.

BACK WAISTLINE

To redraw the back waistline, you will need to proceed in the same way as you did in the front. To adjust and adapt the waist to the shape of the body, lower the waist by 0.5 cm at the center line (Figure 200). Close the dart, pressing its width toward the center, and keep it in that position with a pin.

Using a French curve, positioned as in Figure 201, redraw the waistline.

As with the front, make sure that the angle between the waistline and the center back makes a nice right angle, and do the same with the angle between the waistline and the side line (Figure 202).

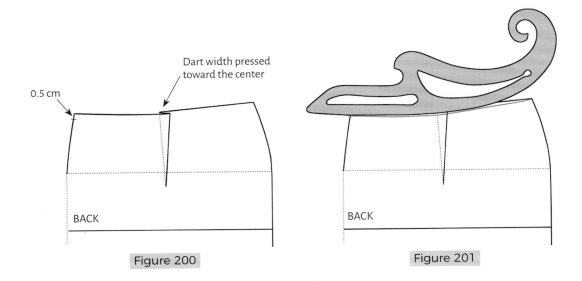

Figure 200

Figure 201

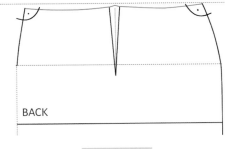

Figure 202

FINISHED BASIC SKIRT PATTERN

On the finished pattern for the basic straight skirt, add the seam allowances. In general, a width of 1 cm is sufficient, but on the fitting pattern, where potential corrections may be applied, plan for a slightly larger allowance.

Add 2 cm of seam allowance on the front and back sides.

So that the skirt can be put on, the length of the opening needs to go a little beyond the full hip line: 0.5 to 1 cm is enough. Then, to make it easier to insert the closure, you can add 2 cm of seam allowance all along the length of the opening.

Don't forget to add the assembly notches.

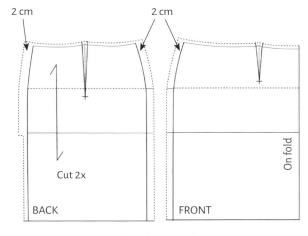

Figure 203

131

CUTTING

You can cut the fitting skirt out of any kind of fabric that has a unified color, with a warp/weft weave, that isn't stretchy, and that is sturdy. One of the best kinds of fabrics to use is a simple muslin.

The front is cut on the fold. Therefore, place the front panel on the fold of the fabric. Then, making sure to observe the straight grain, place the back on the muslin. Anchor the pattern on the fabric using a few pins. Redraw the outline of the pattern, transferring all of the assembly notches.

Then, remove the paper pattern and pin the two layers of the fabric together so that they will not shift during cutting, and, finally, do the cutting.

The fitting muslin should have the construction lines on it: the center front and the full hip line.

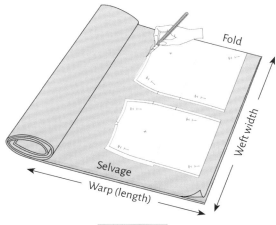

Figure 204

SKIRT ASSEMBLY

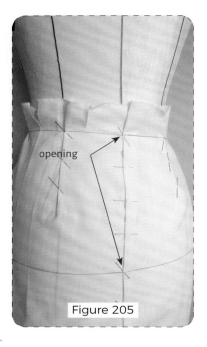

Figure 205

Close up the darts as shown in Figure 113, page 72, then assemble the sides by placing the seam allowances toward the back. Then, pin the center back, as far as the slit for the opening. To facilitate this assembly, place a ruler inside the skirt, as you did with the sleeve assembly (Figure 179, page 112).

A Good Thing to Know

In general, for all skirt designs, any kind of zipper, whether visible or invisible, is placed in the seam at the center back.

It is very rarely placed in the side seam, because the strips of the zipper's spirals, embedded along the straight grain of the closure, could distort the curve of the hip.

The length of the opening needs to go slightly beyond the full hip line, otherwise it will be hard to put the skirt on.

FITTING

Put the skirt on, then close the opening slit on the center back using a few pins, making sure that the full hip lines drawn on each of the half-back skirt panels line up with each other.

First of all, check that the **waist circumference** is correctly adjusted to the body. If it is too big or too small, adjust by either loosening or tightening all of the darts by the same amount so that the balance of the proportions established on the pattern is not thrown off.

Figure 206

POSITIONING THE DARTS

After you adjust the waist circumference, check the **placement of the darts** and look to make sure that the fabric on either side of each dart is not pulling.

If the fabric is not flat in this spot (as can be seen in Figure 207), that means that the dart is too short and too wide. Thus, you will have to make it narrower and transfer the surplus to the next dart or create an additional dart. Check and correct if necessary each of the darts all around the waist.

Also check the placement of each dart. Depending on the body shape, you can change the initial distribution of the dart. This is true in particular for round figures.

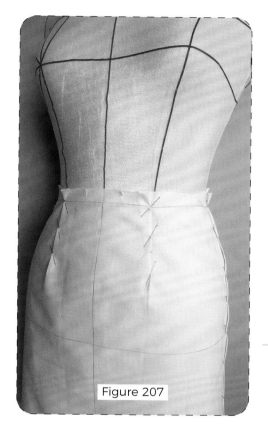

Figure 207

133

DRAPE OF THE SKIRT

Once you have adjusted the width and the height of the darts around the waist, check that the drape of the skirt has not been thrown off. One of the most important steps in the fitting is establishing a good drape for the skirt. This is not simply a question of aesthetics, it also has to do with the comfort of the garment.

A good skirt drape depends on three elements: the center front, the center back, and the side seam line. These lines must therefore be perfectly vertical and parallel, starting from the full hip line.

In general, you adjust the drape by moving the skirt's side seams.

If necessary, then, take out the pins as far as the full hip line, establish a good vertical line, and then repin, maintaining the new line.

PROBLEMS RESULTING FROM THE CONSTRUCTION

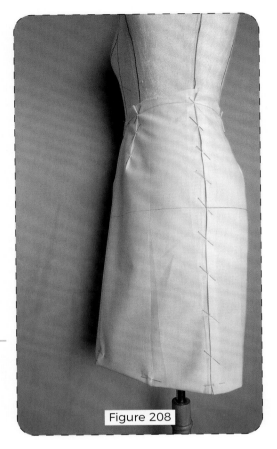

Figure 208

The Front of the Skirt Is Too High

This is the most common issue. It is due to the measurement of the lowering of the waistline (page 129) not matching the shape of the figure.

By looking at the side of the skirt, you can easily see if the front produces a good vertical line or if it tilts. To re-establish the vertical, either raise or lower the waistline in the middle. Place a mark at the waist to indicate the new position of this line, so that you will be able to transfer this correction to the basic paper pattern.

The Back of the Skirt Is Too High

If the center back does not fall vertically, correct it by proceeding in the same way as for the front.

However, this issue, which shows up as a slope in the center, can be more or less of an issue depending on the size of the buttocks. In principle, the waistline is lowered only minimally at the center back, by only 0.5 cm (page 130). Thus, to adjust the drape, for larger body sizes, the waist often needs to be raised above the waist construction line. Place a mark at the waist to indicate the new position of this line so that you will be able to transfer it to the basic paper pattern.

Note

If the front or the back rides too high, this imperfection should never be corrected by changing the line of the bottom of the skirt. That line must always be drawn strictly horizontally.

ADJUSTING THE WAISTLINE

It is very important to adjust the waist line so that it corresponds to the shape of the body, especially for people who have certain curves, for example, a pronounced belly.

If you do not clearly and correctly mark this line on the pattern, the vertical drape of the skirt can be thrown off. This adjustment is essential if the widths of the darts have been changed. Changing the dart widths distorts the waistline as it was planned on the pattern. To correct it, attach a tape measure, a string, or a small cord to the new waistline on the muslin, then, following its position, redraw the waistline.

TRANSFERRING THE CORRECTIONS TO THE PATTERN

The corrections established on the muslin must be transferred to the paper pattern using a colored pencil so that they are clearly visible. Take out the pins to separate the back and the front of the skirt. Also take out the pins that are keeping the darts in place.

Figure 209

Place the muslin back on the paper pattern, first matching up the center back of the muslin with the center back drawn on the paper, and then, in the same way, match up the horizontal construction lines—full hip line and waistline—and then pin them together at each intersection of the center lines with the horizontal lines. Do the same with the front.

Before going on to the next step, make very sure that the muslin pattern is placed perfectly flat against the paper pattern, because the final result depends on this careful placement.

Now transfer to the paper draft the corrections that were made earlier on the muslin: the width and position of the darts, the side line, and the waistline.

Every single mark made on the muslin must absolutely be transferred to the paper. The corrected paper pattern must be identical to the muslin pattern.

Note

You can iron the muslin before cutting it, but never after the fitting, because the heat and steam can change the outline and the shape of the fabric.

PANTS

Drafting a pants pattern based on standard measurements does not generally pose any particular problems. On the other hand, drafting a basic pattern to measure requires more thought and expertise. For this garment, it is easier to adjust it to the particular body shape while trying it on the person directly. Following the shape of the body on the basic pants pattern draft is a delicate exercise that requires a lot of knowledge and skill.

For this complex sewing project, you must carefully follow the instructions given in this chapter and, above all, pay close attention to understanding the explanations about how to draft each line, each curve, and each phase of the work.

Before You Start

To draw the basic pants pattern, prepare a piece of paper as wide as the outline of the half-circumference of the full hips + a margin of about 20 cm, and as long as the leg length of 110 cm + a margin of 5 to 10 cm.

Now take the necessary measurements: waist circumference, full hip circumference, crotch depth, knee length, length to the ground, and the auxiliary measurements for checking the pattern: thigh circumference, calf circumference, and total crotch length (pages 27 to 29).

DRAFTING THE PATTERN

Unlike other patterns (such as the bodice pattern, for example), you can start drafting the basic pants pattern either in the back or the front. This has no effect on the construction, because in the first stages of the drafting, the two panels (back and front) are identical (Figure 188, page 121). The difference between the two begins with the draft of the crotch.

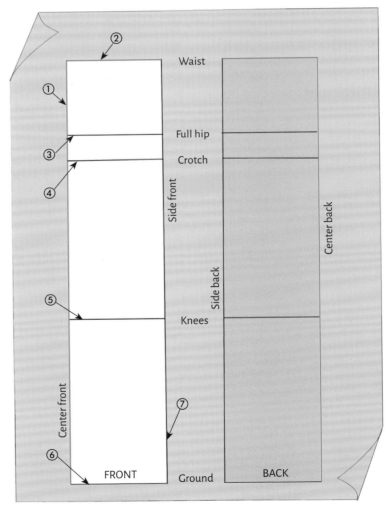

Figure 210

① At about 5 cm from the edge of the paper, draw a long vertical line in red: this is the center front line.

② In red, draw a perpendicular line above the center front line, at about 5 cm from the top edge of the paper: this is the waistline.

③ From the waistline, follow the measurement of the full hip length and at that point draw a line parallel to the waistline, perpendicular to the center front line. This is the full hip line.

④ From the waistline, follow the measurement of the crotch depth (page 28) and at that point draw a line parallel to the waistline, perpendicular to the center front line. This is the crotch line.

⑤ Starting, again from the waistline (which is a reference line), follow the measurement of the knee length and draw a line parallel to the waistline, perpendicular to the center front line. This is the knee line.

⑥ Now draw the last horizontal line: the length of the pants to the ground. This line, like all the others, is drawn by following the measurement of the total length of the pants, starting at the waistline.

⑦ To close up the frame of the half-front outline, measure the full hip circumference and divide that result by 4 (because the pattern is made up of a half-front and a half-back, Figure 11, page 15). Now take that number and follow it along the waistline, starting at the center front line, then at the endpoint of that measurement draw a vertical line down to the end of the pants bottom: this is the side line of the pants.

About 5 to 10 cm from the front side line, draw a mirror image (in blue, Figure 210) of the front outline, by extending all of the horizontal lines and indicating the center back line (in blue) on the right side of the paper.

139

Note

Before going on to the next stage of construction, it is very important to check all of the measurements used here very carefully because the final result depends on this part of the work. A mistake at this stage will make all of the work that follows useless.

PANTS FRONT

FRONT CROTCH WIDTH

① At the level of the center front of the pants, you are going to extend the crotch line by 1/20 of the measurement of the full hip circumference minus 1 cm (short green line on Figure 211).

For example, the full hip circumference is 92 cm; 92 divided by 20 is 4.6 cm, and 4.6 minus 1 is 3.6 cm.

Make this calculation of 1/20th of the measurement of the full hip circumference used to draw your pattern, and extend the crotch line by the resulting length, to the left of the center front line.

CENTRAL CREASE

② The central crease of the pants is at the middle of the total width of the crotch line. Add 1/4 of the full hip circumference to the front crotch width (calculated in point 1 above), then divide the result by 2.

This central crease line becomes a reference line, so it is drawn in red. The center front and center back lines, used to draw the outlines based on the measurements, can be redrawn in black or simply erased.

For example, the full hip circumference is 92 cm; 92 divided by 4 is 23 cm; the front crotch width is 3.6 cm. Thus, the total width of the crotch line is 23 + 3.6, or 26.6 cm, which we divide by 2 to get 13.3 cm.

In this example, the central crease line will be drawn at 13.3 cm from the center front line.

Make the calculation as explained above, starting from the measurements used for your pattern, and then draw the central crease line.

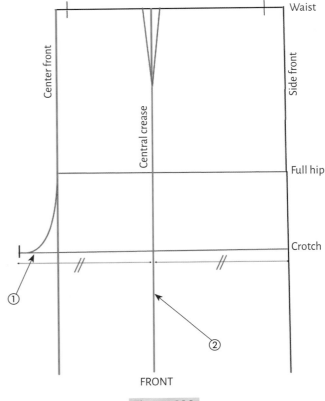

FRONT

Figure 211

DARTS

Center Front Dart

③ This dart is placed more for technical reasons than out of true necessity. It is there to soften the edges of the center front when it is cut on the straight grain. Depending on body shape (for instance in the case of a slightly round belly), this dart can lean either toward the left or the right side of the vertical center line. Measure 1 cm from the center front and, starting from that point, draw a straight line to the full hip (blue line on Figure 212). The width of this dart will be adjusted during fitting.

Waist Darts

④ To determine the widths of the darts placed at the waist on the pants, proceed as you did for the skirt darts or the bodice darts.

For example, full hip circumference = 92 cm; waist circumference = 70 cm. The difference between the two is 22 cm, which we divide by 4, making a total width of 5.5 cm to be absorbed by the darts on each panel. This width of 5.5 cm, in the example given here (Figure 212), should be distributed in a balanced fashion among the side dart (2.5 cm), the dart at the middle of the half-front (2 cm), and the center front dart (1 cm), this last dart already having been established in the previous step.

Now make the calculations based on the measurements used for drafting your pattern and apply them to your outline.

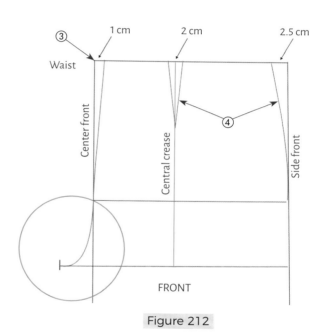

Figure 212

A Good Thing to Know

For the other patterns, the front dart is basically positioned based on the bust-point-to-bust-point measurement. But for the pants pattern, it is often placed on the central crease, creating a harmonious visual effect for the entire pair of pants, with the strong crease. However, it has no effect on the construction or the drape of the pants whether this dart is placed at the bust-point-to-bust-point line or on the central crease.

FRONT CROTCH SHAPE

① At the end of the crotch line, indicate a 1-cm flat area.

② Along the line that bisects the right angle between the center line and the crotch line (thus, at an angle of 45 degrees), follow a 1-to-2 cm measurement (see box opposite) and make a mark at the end of it. Then, using a French curve, draw a curve (blue line on Figure 213) by connecting the following points: the flat area point, the mark placed on the bisecting line, and the full hip width.

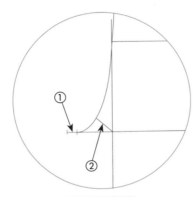

Figure 213

WAISTLINE

Once the dart is closed, the straight line of the waist drawn on the pattern will be disrupted. To adjust it and adapt it to the shape of the body, lower the waist at the center by 1.5 cm (short green line on Figure 214). To redraw the waistline, make sure that the reference lines (in green) are perpendicular (at a 90-degree angle) to the lines that were modified by the darts: the center line and the side line.

Now close the center front dart, pin it to keep it in the closed position, and, using a French curve, redraw the waistline maintaining the right angles at the edges of the half-front.

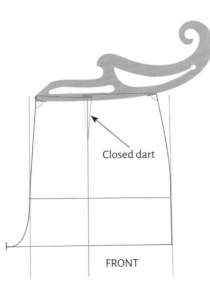

Closed dart

FRONT

Figure 214

PANTS BACK

CENTRAL CREASE

(1) First, draw the central crease on the back pants pattern. To do that, starting at the side line, transfer the measurement that you calculated to find the placement of the front central crease (point 2, page 140). Then, draw a vertical line in red. In the current example, this measurement is 13.3 cm.

Note

The back central crease and the front central crease are both the same distance from the side line.

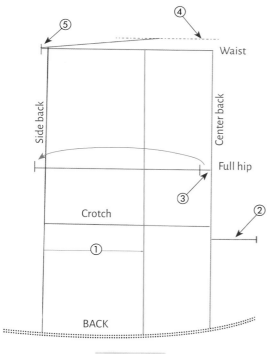

Figure 215

BACK CROTCH

(2) Lower the crotch line by 2 cm. Starting at the center back line, measure 1/20th of the full hip circumference plus 2 cm.

For example, full hip circumference = 92 cm; 1/20th of 92 = 4.6 cm, and if we add 2 cm to that we get 6.6 cm.

Do this calculation, following the full hip circumference used for drawing the pattern. Extend the crotch line by the amount calculated, then make a mark at the end of that line. The 2 cm that are added to the 1/20th of the full hip circumference are a standard number; sometimes you will have to add 3 cm or even 4, depending on the size of the buttocks. This measurement will be accurately defined during the fitting of the pants.

The crotch line, meanwhile, has been lowered by 2 cm, but this measurement rarely needs to be changed. This difference between the two inseam lengths (back and front) provides flexibility along the front of the pants. It is necessary for following the curved shape of the leg and makes the pants more comfortable.

143

③ Along the full hip line, starting at the center back line, place a mark at 2.5 cm. Then extend the full hip line outside the side back line by the same amount (see the red arrow on Figure 215) and make a mark there.

④ Measure 2 cm above the waistline and draw a short line parallel to it, on the side of the center back line. These 2 cm are a minimum measurement, which will depend first on the size of the buttocks, then on the width of the crotch. This measurement is essential for making sure that the waist does not dip down too low when the person leans over or sits down. As with many other measurements for the pants pattern, it will be adjusted and corrected during fitting.

⑤ By tilting the upper part of the pattern (from the crotch to the waist), you will create a space to contain the shape of the buttocks. In order to do this, extend the original waist line by 1.5 cm, outside the side back line. Because this measurement depends on the size of the buttocks, its actual value will be determined during the fitting. Starting at this mark, draw a straight line 1/4th the length of the circumference of the waist, up to the line drawn in point 4 of the construction.

Note

This measurement makes it possible to tilt the center of the pants in such a way as to be able to position the center back dart. The role of this dart is to make the fabric wrap around the buttocks, starting at the beginning of the crotch between the legs and running up to the waistline at the center of the back.

Depending on how large or small the buttocks are, this measurement will increase or decrease. For well-proportioned figures, the tilt of the center back of the pants is between 2 and 3.5 cm.

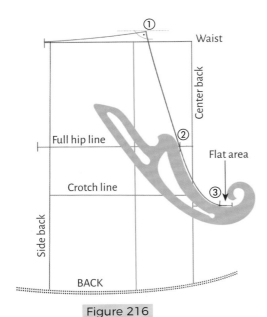

Figure 216

You have now placed all the reference marks you need in order to redefine the center back line of the pants. Draw this new straight line by connecting the endpoint of the line drawn in step 5 above (point 1, Figure 216) with the point placed on the full hip line (green line). Then, indicate the flat area of the crotch: it spans about 1/3 of the total length of the crotch. Make a mark there. Using a French curve, connect the straight line that you just drew with the mark indicating the flat area of the crotch, with a slightly curved line (blue line, Figure 216).

Figure 216 shows how to position the French curve ruler to draw the crotch curve. But in practice you will have to choose the curve on the French curve ruler that best corresponds to your drawing, based on the measurements being used. Make sure to keep the crotch continuous and smooth along its entire length.

HALF-BACK DART

Depending on the body shape of the person or the design of the pants being made, a half-back dart can be established. This dart is not always present and is not always essential to the construction of the basic pattern. Nevertheless, it can improve the aesthetic effect or facilitate the adjustment of the pants to the shape of the figure during the fitting.

To establish the half-back dart, extend the waist circumference line at the center back by the width of the dart. Then redraw the shape of the crotch (blue line, Figure 217) as far as the full hip line. This dart must be placed at the center of the waistline: between the crotch and the side line. First, in the middle of the half-back, draw the axis of the dart with a line perpendicular to the waistline. Then, on either side of this axis, place half the width of the dart. As a reminder, the width of this dart is generally no more than 2 cm (Figure 83, page 55). Don't forget to redraw the waist line once the dart is closed.

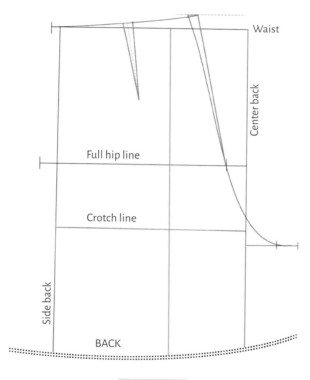

Figure 217

PANTS BOTTOM WIDTH

On the basic pattern, the width of the bottom of the pants is drawn with lines vertical to the floor line, up to the knee line. You can transfer the measurements below to either one of these lines.

You will need to start by determining the width of the bottom of the pants, which cannot be too narrow, to easily locate the drape of the pants: 40 to 44 cm is an average width that can be adapted to all body shapes.

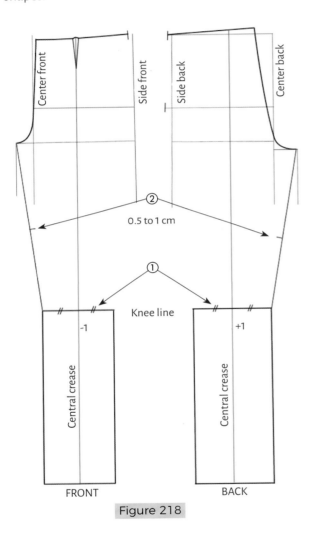

Figure 218

The shape and proportions of the body are such that we must differentiate between the widths of the back and the front.

In general, the back of the pants is wider than the front. This is particularly true for well-proportioned figures. Sometimes the side line is moved toward the front, especially in the case of a prominent belly or rounded thighs. In such a case, this correction will be established during the fitting of the pants.

① Divide the width chosen for the bottom of the pants by 2. Then subtract 1 cm from the front width and add 1 cm to the back width.

For example, if the width of the pants bottom is 40 cm, then 40/2 is 20 cm, and 20 cm minus 1 cm is 19 cm (this is the width of the bottom front of the pants) and 20 cm plus 1 cm is 21 cm (this is the width of the bottom back of the pants).

Then, distribute the widths assigned to the back and the front evenly on either side of the central crease.

In this example, for the front, calculate: 19 cm divided by 2 = 9.5 cm. Transfer this measurement to either side of the central crease line. Then, at the end of the measurement on each side, draw the vertical lines from the knee line to the floor line.

Do the same thing for the back: 21 cm divided by 2 = 10.5 cm. Transfer this measurement to either side of the central crease line. Then, at the end of the measurement on each side, draw the vertical lines from the knee line to the floor line.

② Draw straight lines to connect the ends of the crotches (of the back and of the front) to the ends of the leg widths at the level of the knees (green lines, Figure 218). Then, in the middle of each of the straight lines that you just drew, place a short perpendicular line between 0.5 and 1 cm long. In practice, this measurement will depend on the body shape or the circumference of the thigh (page 148).

DRAWING THE OUTLINES OF THE PANTS

The final step in constructing the basic pants pattern involves finishing the complete outline of the back and the front. Use a straight ruler and a French curve to connect the reference marks placed during the preceding steps. The lines that you draw must be smooth with gentle curves and no visible gaps or bumps. In Figure 219, the positions of the French curve are just indications; they will have to be adapted depending on the measurements you use.

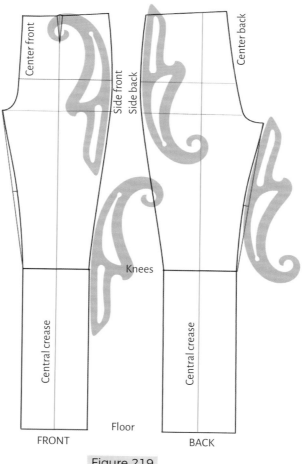

Figure 219

CHECKING THE PATTERN

APPLYING THE MEASUREMENTS

The basic pants pattern draft is now finished. But even if it was carried out with the utmost precision, you will have to check the body measurements that were not taken into account for the construction (such as the thigh circumference), as well as how the edges match up—make sure that they do not create either sagging or bulging lines.

THIGH CIRCUMFERENCE

The measurement of the thigh circumference taken from the figure (Figure 40, page 27) is very important, especially if the person has well-developed thighs. The pants will be adjusted to the shape of the legs during the fitting, but you still need to check whether the width defined on the pattern corresponds to the actual measurement.

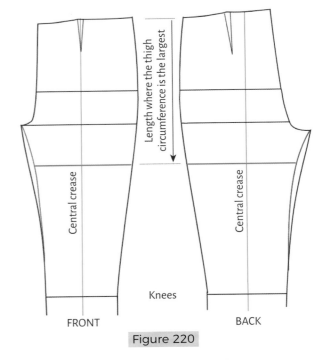

Figure 220

To do this, start by finding the length at which the thigh circumference is the greatest, starting from the waist. Transfer this length to the pattern (black arrow, Figure 220), Then, at the indicated length, measure the total width of the leg: back + front.

As an example, in Figure 220, the blue lines indicate where you will have to measure the leg circumference (from the pattern). In general, this measurement taken from the pattern will be equal to or greater than the actual measurement taken on the person's body.

Divide the thigh circumference by 2. Then, transfer this measurement to the line that has been drawn for the thigh circumference on the front. Place a mark at the endpoint of this measurement.

Now redraw the inseam line with a slight curve, passing through this mark (Figure 220).

The second half of the thigh circumference measurement is transferred to the back pattern in the same way as on the front.

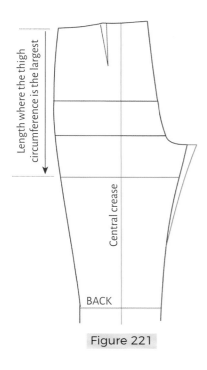

Length where the thigh circumference is the largest

Central crease

BACK

Figure 221

It very rarely happens that the thigh circumference measurement taken from the figure is larger than the measurement established on the pattern draft. But if that does happen and the difference is between 1 and 2 cm, then extend the crotch width by 1 to 2 cm and redraw the inseam line (green line, Figure 221). On the other hand, if the difference is greater than that, there has probably been a mistake in the draft. In that case, you will need to revisit your measurements and how they have been applied to the draft.

CROTCH LENGTH

On the pattern, the crotch is made up of two parts: the back and the front. The measure taken from the figure includes the entire length of the crotch, in other words both parts (Figure 42, page 28). To check the length of the crotch, you will thus have to add the measurements of the two crotch lengths (back [blue line] and front [green line, Figure 222]) as defined on the pattern. In general, there is a difference of a few centimeters between the total crotch measurement on the pattern and that measured

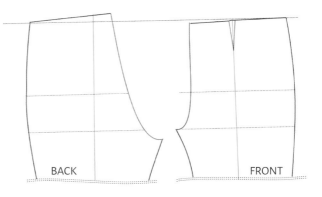

BACK

FRONT

Figure 222

from the figure. This is often due to an inaccuracy when taking the measurement from the person's body (page 27) because when making this measurement, you generally ignore the size of the buttocks.

If the difference between the two measurements is no more than 5 to 7 cm, you can correct this during the fitting. If, on the other hand, the difference is greater than that, you have most likely made a mistake at some point in applying the measurements to the pattern. Check your draft to find where the error was introduced. Very often, the center back is not raised up high enough (Figure 215, page 143) to encompass the size of the buttocks.

BASIC ENLARGEMENTS

In every pattern draft, whether it is a basic pattern or a finished garment pattern, there are a variety of enlargements. These additions to the measurements are necessary and will vary depending on the style of the garment, the thickness of the fabric, or individual preferences (including how loose the garment is).

The measurements that are added to the basic pattern are minimal and only correspond to the thickness of the seam allowances. They are only rarely used for drafting garment patterns. The enlargements for the basic pants pattern consist of increasing the measurements in height and width. It is important to plan for these enlargements, because without them you will get pants that are too tight, impossible to put on (and therefore to try on), and you will thus not be able to check the adjustment to the body nor judge whether the fabric has a good drape.

① Raise the waistline by 2 cm. This enlargement will allow you to correctly adjust and to redraw the waist-line during the fitting. This line, which was already modified after the darts were closed (Figure 214, page 142), will need to be modified again in order to be adapted to the body shape. This 2-cm margin added to the height will also ensure a comfortable fit in the crotch (so that it is neither too tight nor too low).

② Enlarge the waistline along the side back and the side front by 0.25 cm (1 cm adjusted along the entire waist circumference, divided by 4). As a general rule, whether we are talking about skirts or pants, the waist circumference measurement must be consistently enlarged by 1 cm to absorb the thickness of the fabric. Because the belt (or any other edge finish at the waistline) has several layers of fabric, the garment will be too tight at the waist without this addition of 1 cm.

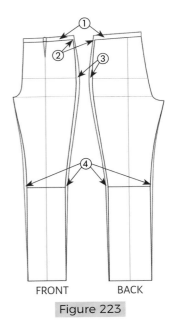

FRONT   BACK

Figure 223

③ Extend the full hip line by 1 cm along the side back and the side front, which means that overall, you are enlarging the full hip circumference by 4 cm (1 cm per panel). This enlargement is not essential; you will add it or not depending on the design, the thickness of the fabric, and individual preferences. In the case of a draft made to measure, it will be corrected and adjusted to the body shape during the fitting.

Now draw the enlargement line along the side front and side back lines of the pants (green line, Figure 223), by connecting the marks placed at the level of the waistline and the full hip line. This line ends at the knees, but do not end it abruptly. It should disappear progressively around the knee line, reconnecting with the line marking the pants width right around that height. This new line should be nice and smooth, without any bumps or bulges, along its entire length.

④ When drawing the enlargement line, you must maintain the proportions established during the drafting process. Make sure that the lengths that appear at the ends of the knee line, between the draft line (in black) and the enlargement line (in blue and green), are exactly equal on the back and front legs.

MATCHING UP THE EDGES

After checking the measurements that were not involved in the construction of the pattern (thigh circumference and calf circumference), you will have to check the places where the edges meet up so as not to have any unpleasant surprises during the assembly or the fitting.

All of the lines where the edges of the pants pieces join up (side back with side front, center back, back crotch with front crotch, etc.) must be continuous and smooth, with no gaps, hollows, bulges, or misalignments.

Note

The connections between the edges of the pattern draft should be checked after the enlargements have been applied, but always before the seam allowances are added.

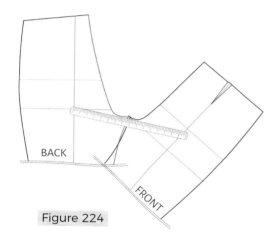

Figure 224

FLAT AREA AT THE CROTCH

The shape of the inseam lines is slightly curved. When you are matching up the edges of the crotch and the inseam, a small "beak" often appears at the assembly point. This is due to the slope of the inseam line, which does not form a right angle (90 degrees). In order to correct this imperfection on the pattern draft, match up the two inseam edges in such a way that the back crotch (in blue) and the front crotch (in black) are at the same level (Figure 224). Then, using a ruler, draw a short straight line to connect the flat areas of the two crotch curves.

Now cut away the excess, following the line you have drawn. The new line that makes up the entirety of the crotch (the back and front parts together) must be smooth and continuous along all of its length, with no gaps, hollows, bulges, or misalignments.

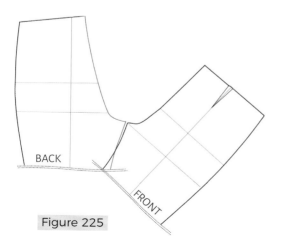

Figure 225

CHECKING THE WAISTLINE

During the different phases of drafting the pattern, the waistline is redrawn, moved, or modified, because of the application of the steps of the drafting, the placement of the darts at the waist, and the addition of the enlargements. You have to make sure there are no hollows, bulges, or misalignments anywhere along its total length. This check is made in several steps: at the sides (Figure 226), the center back (Figure 227), and the center front (Figure 228). Match up each element with the one that corresponds to it, making the construction lines (hip, crotch) connect, and check the connection at the waistline using the French curve. If necessary, redraw the waistline so that it is perfectly smooth and continuous, with no distortions or misalignments.

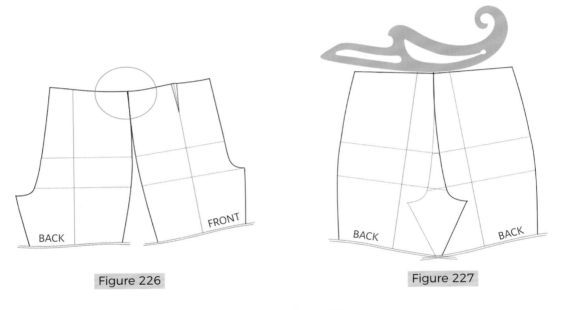

Figure 226

Figure 227

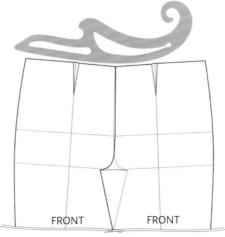

Figure 228

SEAM ALLOWANCE

Generally speaking, the seam allowance is planned as 1 cm; this is the width that is best adapted to assembling garments. But because you will probably be making some corrections to the fitting pattern, you can increase this allowance up to 2 cm. This will make the adjustment easier in case you have to enlarge or move the construction line on the muslin. This is particularly necessary for fitting pants made to measure. The crotch is a relatively complex element to draw correctly and it is rare for it not to have to be adjusted during the fitting.

All around the outline of the back and the front, add the seam allowance (dotted black line, Figure 229), making sure to take the already-planned enlargement into account (green line).

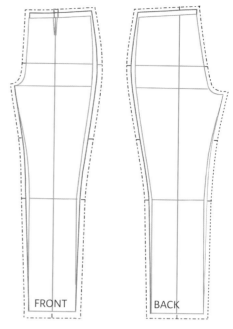

Figure 229

CUTTING

153

The fitting pattern must be cut from a fabric that is not easily distorted and does not stretch. The most suitable fabric is a warp/weft weave in a neutral color (so that the correction marks are clearly visible), a muslin that is also often used for draping.

Fold the fabric in half, so that the two panels (left and right) will be completely identical. Position the pattern in such a way as to respect the straight grain (the straight grain is parallel to the selvage). Pin the

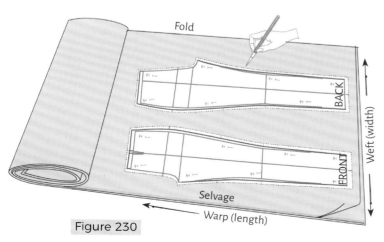

Figure 230

pattern to the fabric in several spots, then trace the outline using a piece of chalk or a pencil. Transfer the widths and lengths of the darts (Figure 111, page 70) as well. Now remove the paper pattern, pin the two layers of fabric inside the outlines of the pattern so that they will be kept in position, and then cut along the lines. Before removing the pins, check the notches placed along the edges of the pattern.

ASSEMBLY

When you assemble the elements that make up the pants, you must take into account the seam allowance widths and make sure the assembly notches match up correctly. The inseam and side seams should be pressed toward the back. To make this easier, you can flatten the seam allowances ahead of time (Figure 119, page 76).

A Good Thing to Know

In general, fitting patterns are assembled using pins to have quick and easy access to the seams in case of corrections.

But for safety reasons (to avoid having the person get pricked by the pins), some pants seams are assembled using a basting stitch. This is the case for the assembly along the entire length of the crotch (back and front) and for part of the inseam seam. To make a correction along one of these parts, you will have to mark the proper positions on the muslin, take the pants off, undo the basting stitch, make the correction, and then re-baste the pants and put them back on again in order to see if the correction is accurate.

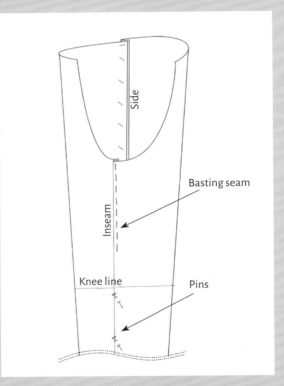

SIDE SEAM

Assemble the elements of each leg separately, the back with the front. Start with the side seam, and press seam allowances toward the back. Use the technique described on page 72 (Figure 1): fold the back seam allowance, lay it on top of the front seam allowance, then pin them together.

INSEAM SEAM

Close up the pants leg. To avoid pulling the fabric that is underneath into this seam, place a hard item like a board or just a ruler in between the two layers of the muslin (Figure 231). First, connect the edges using pins, and then, on the section from the crotch to the knee line, baste the edges together. For the rest of the seam, from the knee line to the floor, you can just pin the seam.

CROTCH SEAM

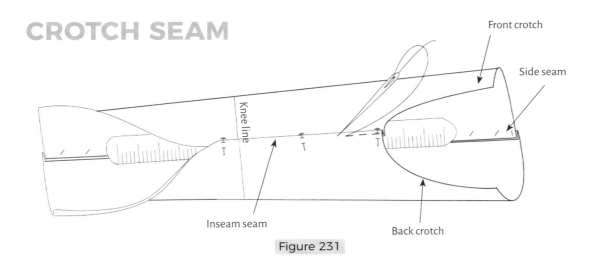

Figure 231

Complete the pants assembly by making the two legs of the pants. So that the person does not get pricked during the fitting, baste the crotch seam by hand.

Maintain the length of the opening in the center front and the seam allowances. Match up the notches and the inseam seams.

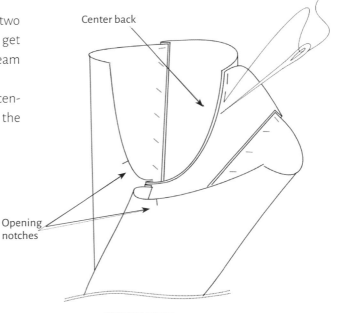

Figure 232

FITTING

The most important element during the cutting of the pants is the shape of the crotch.

A crotch curve that is not well-matched to the shape of the body will both make the pants uncomfortable and destroy the aesthetic effect because of the creases that will form around the crotch in front or in back, and the drape of the pants can also be thrown off (if the central crease does not fall vertically).

Not only is adjusting the crotch of the pants to the body shape a very precise job, but it also requires a certain amount of experience to locate the origins of the problem and to correct it appropriately. To succeed in this step, follow all of the instructions described here very carefully, which will allow you to understand which correction to apply depending on the problem that you have found.

BEFORE PUTTING ON THE FITTING PANTS

After you have assembled the elements of the pants, and before you have put them on the model make any necessary corrections after doing a preliminary check. Fold both legs along the central crease and place the pants on a flat surface. The seams of the two legs should be lying exactly on top of each other, without producing either extra fabric or wrinkles. If this is not the case, check the width of the seam allowance that you used to assemble the legs along the side and the inseam. If everything is correct in those places, check the widths of the legs on the back and front on the draft pattern.

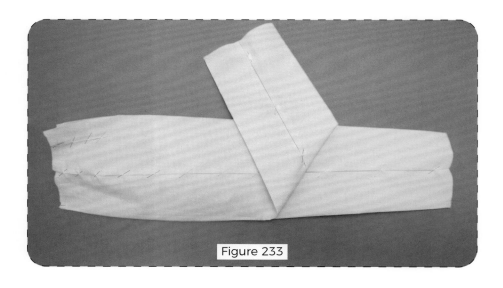

Figure 233

DRAPE OF THE PANTS

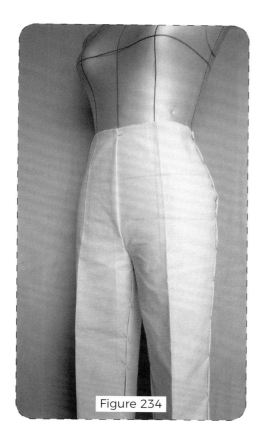

Figure 234

In a well-constructed pair of pants, the line of the central crease, from the waist down to the bottom of the pants, must be continuous, without breaks or interruptions at any point along the entirety of its length. Even if the future design of the pants does not include this clearly marked crease, the fitting pants must include it. This continuity of the central crease line also indicates that the crotch curve was drawn correctly on the pattern. If there is any problem in the crotch, it will have a direct impact on the vertical line of the central crease. However, if there is a problem with how the vertical central crease line falls, it can be caused by many other things—for instance, if the legs have a particular shape (such as knock knees).

Correcting the fitting pattern takes place in two stages, during which you will pay attention mostly to the crotch and to the drape of the central crease.

In practice, a poorly adjusted crotch can have an impact on the vertical drape of the pants, but the converse is not the case: the vertical drape has no impact on the crotch. To effectively correct the fitting pattern, you will need to find the origin of the problem.

Figure 235

BACK CROTCH

It is not easy to correctly draw the back crotch curve when drafting a pattern to measure, because the shape of this curve must correspond exactly to the shape of the buttocks. If there is any kind of wrinkle or an interruption of the central crease below the buttocks, or there is gaping at the level of the full hip line (Figure 236), you will first have to check whether the pants are wide enough at the full hip line. Sometimes too much or too little enlargement produces this effect.

But in most cases, the problem is that the crotch curve is not deep enough. To fix this, pin the crotch seam, starting at the bottom of the crotch, and increase the seam allowance until the wrinkle completely disappears (Figure 237). Then mark the placement on the muslin, using a pencil and following the pins (this will make it easier to correct the paper pattern).

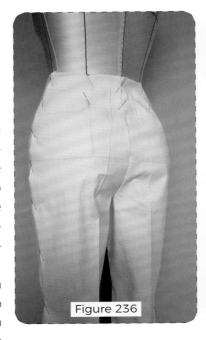

Figure 236

Figure 237

Transferring the Corrections to the Pattern

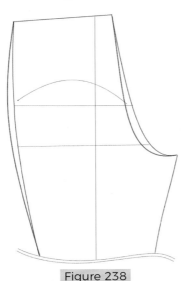

Figure 238

Measure the width of the seam allowance determined during the fitting, then transfer this value to the pattern. Now redraw the shape of the crotch seam (see the example in green, Figure 238). Because the crotch curve has been made deeper, the full hip width has been reduced. Above all, do not forget to restore this measurement to what it was to begin with.

FRONT CROTCH

Problems that appear on the front crotch (Figure 239) can have several different causes. The most common is the shape of the center front opening slit. On the pattern, the front vertical line is tilted inward by 1 cm, but in practice, this tilt depends on body shape (based on how rounded the belly is).

First, correct the slope of the edges of the opening. This will allow you to nicely flatten the fabric in the upper part of the crotch. Proceed in the same way as for the back: take out the pins that are holding the opening slit and adjust the muslin around it until the wrinkles disappear entirely. If you do this, any gaping and any interruption of the central crease line should disappear. Then position the marks on the fabric, following the pins, which show the new slope of the opening slit.

If, in spite of all this, there are still wrinkles around the lower part of the crotch, this means that the crotch curve is too deep. In that case you will have to redraw it, making it shallower (green line, Figure 241).

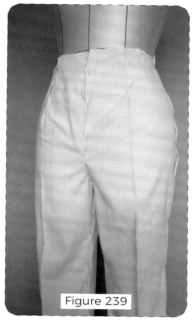

Figure 239

Figure 240

159

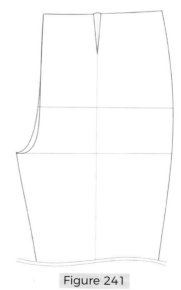

Figure 241

The flaws you see can have other causes as well. If there are wrinkles, and they are pulling horizontally on the lower part of the crotch, that means that the shape of the crotch is too deep and often also too short. This will cause significant discomfort when walking or sitting. Correcting this type of problem must be done in two steps: first start by fixing the crotch curve, and then, if necessary (which it not always is), shortening it.

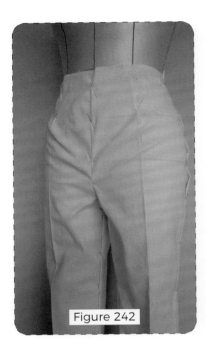

Figure 242

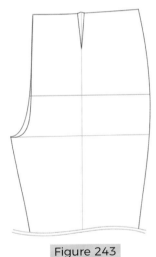

Figure 243

This problem cannot be corrected while the pants are being worn. You will have to undo the assembly seam, add a small piece of muslin (assemble it flat so you won't have the thickness of the seam allowances [Figure 132, page 82]), and then redraw a shallower curve (green line, Figure 243). Redo your baste stitch and put the pants back on the model.

In principle, this change should address the problem. If there is still an awkward fit in the crotch or there are still wrinkles, you will then have to lengthen the crotch by 1 to 2 cm (Figure 244).

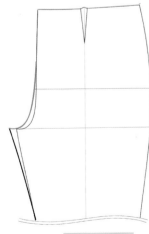

Figure 244

MOST COMMON PROBLEMS

CONSTRAINING CROTCH SEAM

It often happens that the front and back crotch are correctly constructed, the central creases have the right vertical drape, but the crotch seam is too tight and hinders every movement of the body. To fix this problem, you will have to make the crotch slightly deeper.

To do this, place the back and front patterns face to face, lengthen the back crotch curve by 1 to 2 cm, and redraw the entire curve (front and back) lowered by about 1 cm (green curve, Figure 245).

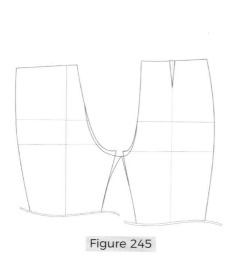

Figure 245

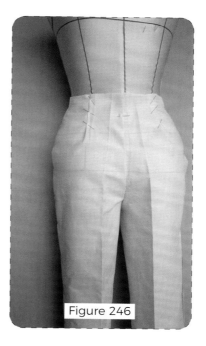

Figure 246

161

A Good Thing to Know

If the crotch seam is constraining, simply adding 1 to 2 cm above the waistline will not fix the problem. Because if the placement of the waist is changed, then the full hip line, the crotch line, the knee line, and the shape of the side line will all have to be moved as well. It's much easier just to redraw the crotch curve.

CENTRAL CREASE

Adjusting the crotch (which is the first thing that you will correct during the fitting) can have a direct effect on the vertical drape of the central crease. The corrections made to the crotch often cause the drape of the central crease to automatically adjust itself all along its length, but sometimes it only adjusts itself on the upper part of the pants (down to the knee line). If the vertical line of the central crease is thrown off starting at the waist, you will have to revisit the construction of the pattern (Figure 211, page 140). If, on the other hand, it is only thrown off starting around the knee line and from there to the bottom of the pants, this could also have to do with the person's body shape or the shape of their legs.

Central Crease Turning Inward

If the central crease is turning inward, you must first define, on the front bottom of the pants, the correct placement of the crease. Starting at that point, draw a vertical line until it connects with the flattened fold that is already on the fabric (green line, Figure 247A). Also mark the height at which they connect (dotted black line). Now transfer the corrections made on the fabric to the paper pattern (green line, Figure 247B). Then measure the difference between the existing fold (in red, Figure 247A) and the corrected line (in green), and then transfer this width to the outside of the inseam construction line to shift the width of the bottom of the pants toward the outside (in blue, Figure 247B), paying attention to the height at which this correction occurs (dotted black line between Figures 247 A and B).

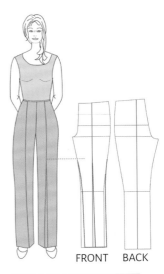

Figures 247 A and B

FRONT   BACK

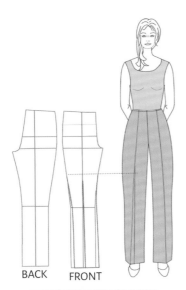

BACK   FRONT

Figures 248 A and B

Central Crease Turning Outward

If the central crease is turning outward, the method for shifting the width of the bottom of the pants is the same as that used for a crease turning inward. Therefore, proceed as described in the previous paragraph. But instead of shifting the width of the bottom toward the outside, shift it toward the inside (in blue, Figure 248A). If, on the back of the pants, the vertical crease does not fall vertically along the bottom part of the pants, then proceed in the same way as for the front.

SIDE LINE

Figure 249

After adjusting the crotch and the drape of the central crease, you need to focus on the side line seam. Whatever corrections you make on the fitting muslin, you must never throw off the vertical line of the side seam.

To make sure that this line has an accurate drape, you can simply eyeball it; if that isn't enough, then attach a not-too-heavy weight (such as an L-square or a small chisel) to the end of a long string, and suspend it from the full hip line. If the string is perfectly parallel with the side line seam, then the seam is correctly positioned. If the string does not fall parallel to the seam line, then mark the correct placement with a pencil and redo the seam, following the new drawing.

WAISTLINE

Adjusting the waistline is the last correction to be made to the fitting pattern, after having corrected the crotch, the central lines, and the side lines, one after the other.

Unlike the side line, the waist line cannot be corrected by eyeing it alone. Tie a string or a tape measure to the waist, making sure that it is correctly positioned, especially for round figures or body shapes with prominent bellies. Draw the shape made by the string or tape all around the waist, using a pencil.

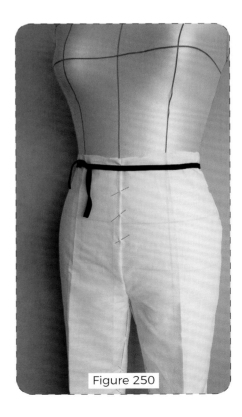

Figure 250

ADAPTING THE DRAFT TO THE BODY SHAPE

Certain body shape particularities, in particular a rounded belly or prominent buttocks, can be dealt with directly when drafting the pattern. In practice, it is impossible to make precise measurements of the size and shape of these parts of the body. Thus, it is wise to take the necessary steps at the beginning, when drafting the paper pattern, so that correcting the fitting pattern later on will be easier.

ROUNDED BELLY

This can be taken into account during the drafting of the basic pattern in two ways (Figure 252 or Figure 253). The choice between the two depends on the shape and, even more so, the size of the belly. Thus, you will need to carefully observe the figure so that you can decide which of the two solutions is more appropriate.

If the figure is obese or very stout, with a prominently rounded belly, you have no choice but to adapt the basic pattern, because the standard construction will not correspond to this kind of body shape. Of course, you can also make adjustments during the fitting, but this requires a certain expertise. To avoid this difficulty, a small manipulation in the front section is required. You will need one additional measurement: the front width along the upper hip line (Figure 52, page 37).

Figure 251

Beginning at the center front (in red, Figure 252), along the upper hip line (dotted black line), transfer half the measurement of the front width, and place a mark at the endpoint of that measurement. To more easily shift the upper part of the pattern, copy the waistline and the side line down to the full hip line, using tracing paper. Then pivot the copy, at the point where the side line and the full hip line intersect, until the shifted side line touches the point that you have just marked on the upper hip line. Then, increase the height of the waistline at the center front by 0.5 to 1 cm. The waistline and its darts will also get shifted (in blue, Figure 252).

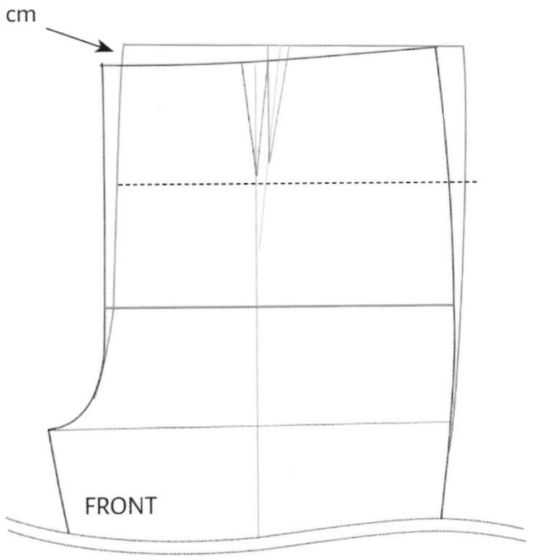

0.5 to 1 cm

FRONT

Figure 252

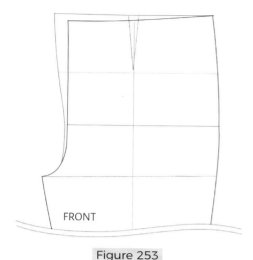

Figure 253

On the other hand, if the figure is less rounded and the belly less prominent, it is enough to just increase the front width. On the pattern draft, shift the center front line by 1 to 2 cm toward the outside (in blue, Figure 253 and page 141, "Center front dart") and increase it upward slightly (0.5 to 1 cm is enough). In this case, the position of the waist dart will be adjusted during the fitting.

PROMINENT BUTTOCKS

The basic back pattern can be modified in such a way as to take the size of the buttocks (and thus the measurement of their contour) into account; however, their shape cannot be addressed except through an adjustment during the fitting process.

Start by widening the crotch by about 1 to 2 cm and slightly lowering it, then redraw the depth of this new crotch beginning at the crotch line (in blue, Figure 251). Also increase the height of the waistline by 1 or possibly 2 cm (the exact width will be dictated by the fitting). Shift the front part of the pants until it touches the increased waistline (in green, Figure 255). To make this easier and to help you ensure that it is accurate, redraw the relevant elements using tracing paper: the side line, the waistline, and the crotch to the crotch line. Then shift the tracing, balanced along the exterior point of the knee line.

Figure 254

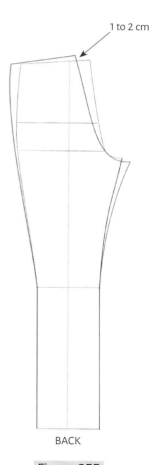

1 to 2 cm

BACK

Figure 255

MANIPULATING THE BASIC PATTERN

We generally call it manipulating the pattern when the basic pattern (the outline of the figure, drawn flat on paper) is modified to obtain a desired design.

Remember that every modification, whether simple or complex, that is transferred to the basic pattern transforms it into a finished pattern to be used for cutting. To understand and be successful at this phase of the work, you will need to follow all of the steps and rules for the manipulation described in this chapter.

Before You Start

Of the different kinds of patterns (basic pattern, fitting pattern, modified pattern, or finished pattern), it is the basic pattern (drawn without any enlargements and without the seam allowances) to which you will apply the necessary modifications to produce a finished pattern for the design.

The virtual lines of the body (upper chest, waist, full hip, etc.) that are drawn on the pattern play a fundamental role in all of the manipulations. It is on these lines that that you will indicate a new position for the darts, where to make a cut, or the starting point for a flare of the vertical line—depending on the desired design—so that the construction will not be thrown off.

Any basic pattern at all, whether it is for the bodice, the skirt, the sleeve, or the pants, can be manipulated, as long as you follow certain essential rules, such as the width of the darts or the vertical drape of the garment.

The manipulations applied to the basic pattern can be simple or very complex. The degree of difficulty depends not just on your level of knowledge about pattern making but also on the type of garment design (simple or elaborate) as well as, and especially, on your ability to analyze the design and plan the order of the steps in the manipulation.

(1) First of all, you will need to choose the pattern that is best adapted to the design: with or without the basic darts.

(2) Then, you will add the enlargements that are necessary for the design you are making.

(3) Next, you will apply the modifications, depending on the design: for example, drawing the cut lines, moving the darts, indicating any facings, positioning pockets or yokes, etc.

(4) Using carbon paper, tracing paper, or a tracing wheel, individually copy all of the elements drawn on the pattern in the previous step.

(5) Check all of the elements that make up the pattern, including the length of the edges, the notches, the positioning of the straight grain, the labels, etc.

(6) Finally, apply the seam allowances.

ENLARGEMENTS

Any enlargements absolutely must appear on the basic pattern. This is the first step in applying the modifications to the basic pattern.

Aside from the minimal enlargements made to the fitting pattern (see page 66), there is no reference list or chart that will tell you the measurements for the enlargements added to each style and kind of garment.

The size of the enlargements will vary, depending on several different criteria:

- The style of garment: shirt, coat, jacket, etc.
- The nature and quality of the fabric: fine, thick, fluid, elastic
- Finally—and these are the most important criteria—comfort and personal taste

INCREASING THE HEIGHT

Shoulder length

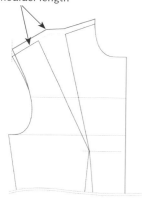

Figure 256

This enlargement is not always applied. Whether it is or not depends on the thickness of the fabric being used, when making clothes that are fairly fitted.

In the case of a lined jacket, for example, you will need to use the complete pattern, including the basic darts, to apply the manipulations. On that pattern, the height of the bust point is clearly indicated (bust length line, Figure 21, page 20). But if you do not add at least 1 cm in height (green line, Figure 256) to accommodate the thickness of the seam allowances of the fabric and the facing, and to respect the fact that there needs to be space between the skin and the garment to provide a certain level of comfort, then, on a ready-made garment, the bust length line will rise. And as a result, the curve of the bust will be distorted and not where it should be.

In Figure 256, therefore, it is necessary to add height.

On the other hand, in the case of a flared jacket cut out of a thick fabric, where you are going to apply the modifications to the basic pattern, not including the darts (Figure 138, page 87), it is not necessary to increase the height. In this kind of design (Figure 257), neither the waist nor the bust length is marked.

It is, however, essential to make enlargements to the width.

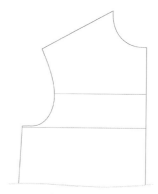

Figure 257

INCREASING THE WIDTH

As much as it is optional to increase the height, it is absolutely necessary to increase the width in every case. Regardless of the design and style of the garment, you must enlarge the width.

Even if the criteria for enlargement are technically very clear (thickness of the fabric, seam allowances, etc.), there is always some hesitation over exactly how much to enlarge by. How much extra width needs to be given to a skirt, a dress, a coat, a pair of pants, or a jacket so that it will be neither too loose nor too tight? Aside from the technical criteria, the parameters that are involved in creating the esthetic effect and the comfort of the garment are the most important ones.

For a slightly figure-hugging dress, for example (green line, Figure 258): The armhole, starting at the upper chest line, will be lowered by 1 cm. Beyond 1 cm, when the person moves their arms, the sleeve might cause the dress to rise too much. The full bust circumference should be enlarged by about 4 cm, the waist circumference by 4 to 6 cm, and the full hip circumference by enough (as much as or more than the waist circumference) so that the dress will fall naturally thanks to the weight of the fabric.

In Figure 258, as an example, we show the enlargement for a loosely belted coat (blue line). The shoulder length and the upper chest width have been extended by 1 to 2 cm and the armhole has been lowered by 3 to 5 cm. At the level of the full bust circumference, you will add 8 to 10 cm; on a coat that has a straight shape, this measurement is retained all the way to the bottom of the garment, and otherwise, this line will be flared to the desired width for the design.

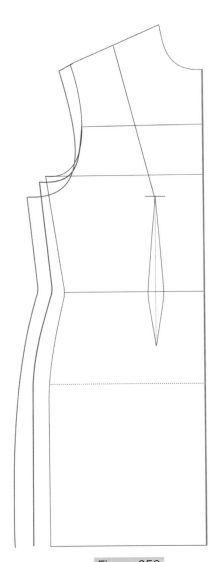

Figure 258

On the other hand, if the bodice hangs loose from the front shoulder level (dotted green line, Figure 259), lift the armhole by about 1 cm starting at the upper chest line. In this kind of design, the armhole is not held in place at the shoulder and can easily fall, especially if the garment is cut out of a fluid fabric such as crepe.

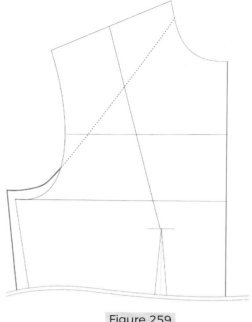

Figure 259

In the case of garments that are restrained at the waist, like skirts or pants, you will very seldom add width at the waist. When you do, it won't be more than a total of 1 cm for the entire circumference.

However, at the full hip level more enlargement will be needed in order to move the legs and buttocks comfortably: in general, the minimum amount for this enlargement is 4 cm for the entire circumference of the full hips.

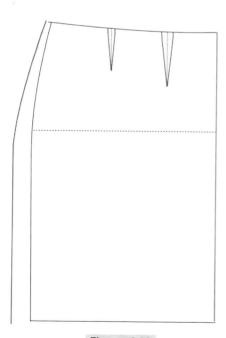

Figure 260

MODIFYING Patterns

After you have added the enlargements to the basic pattern, you can start to apply the manipulation, according to the design you are going to make. As you have already seen, this manipulation must follow a few rules, which are not all the same for the bodice, pants, skirt, or sleeve.

This is why each of these elements will be addressed separately in the context of manipulating the basic pattern.

MANIPULATING THE BODICE

Almost all of the manipulations applied to the basic bodice pattern, such as the placement of the cut lines or of the darts, are dependent on the bust point, which is determined according to two measurements: the bust length (page 20) and the bust-point-to-bust-point distance (page 21).

Whatever manipulation is being applied to the bodice, the front shoulder dart is the element that plays the most important role. Depending on the desired design, this dart is not necessarily maintained at its usual position (on the shoulder). It is often moved to a cut line or pivoted to another spot.

There is a very simple technique that allows you to move the front shoulder dart to any position around the bust point.

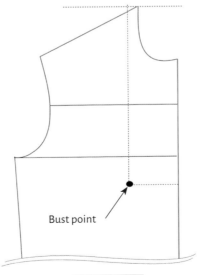

Bust point

Figure 261

PIVOTING THE DARTS

The most appropriate and most commonly used technique for moving darts is cutting. This is done in two steps:

- The first step is to mark the new position of the dart. To do this, draw a straight line from the bust point to the edge of the pattern in any direction. Then make a cut as far as the bust point, following the line you just drew.
- In the second step, you will have to close up the front shoulder dart: The width of this dart will shift toward the cutout that you made in the first step.

Armhole Dart

A front shoulder dart placed within the armhole and connected to the waist dart results in a cutout called a "princess dart." Pattern makers often use this cut because it can be easily adapted to all body shapes.

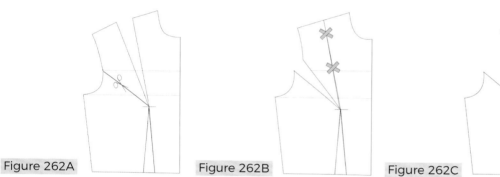

Figure 262A   Figure 262B   Figure 262C

To move the front shoulder into the armhole:

- Draw the new position of the dart (green line, Figure 262A), and then cut
- Close up the front shoulder dart using tape (Figure 262B) to subtract its width
- Separate the two front parts, round out the bust point, and make very sure to keep the bust notches on both parts (Figure 262C). They will be essential during the assembly.

The position of the front shoulder dart in the armhole must be very precise, both aesthetically and technically.

In general, this dart starts at the level of the upper chest line (green line, Figure 262A). If it is placed lower than that, in other words in the armhole curve, the following seams (the dart and facing or sleeve assembly seams) might distort this part of the bodice. Another reason not to position the dart within the armhole curve is that this would make the bodice too pointy. On the other hand, putting this dart above the upper chest line is not a terrible thing to do technically, but it would have unpleasant aesthetic repercussions: it would flatten the bust and lengthen the lower part of the bodice.

Side Dart

This dart can be placed anywhere along the length of the side line, starting at the armhole and going down to the full hip line (dotted blue lines, Figure 263). However, to avoid an overlap with the seam allowances, you must maintain a distance of at least 3 cm below the armhole curve.

The disadvantage of placing this dart between the waist and the full hip line is that there is a large amount of fabric at the hip line. But the huge aesthetic upside is that it will very effectively hide a belly that is a little too prominent and will also emphasize the waist.

Draw a straight line from the bust point to the side line at the desired position (for example the green line, Figure 263), and then cut.

Close up the front shoulder dart using tape (Figure 264).

On the design shown here, the waist dart was not taken into account, but it can be retained, or, in the case of well-developed figures, half of its width can be added to the side dart.

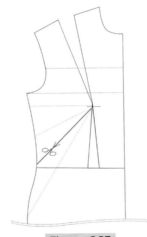

Figure 263

Figure 264

Bust Dart

This dart is always placed on a V-neck or on a cut line in the center front. These two elements are linked to the slope of the center line after the bust dart is opened. This dart can take the form of folds or of vertical gathers.

Draw a line to position the dart between the center front and the bust point (green line, Figure 265A), then cut.

Close up the front shoulder dart and hold it in place using a pin or tape. The bust dart will open naturally (Figure 265B).

In Figures 265 A and B, the waist dart is kept open, but to increase the width of the bust dart, the waist dart can also be closed (Figure 265C).

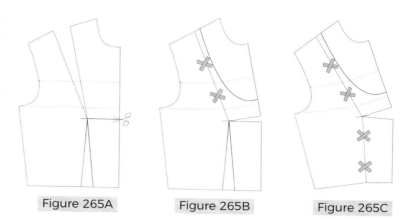

Figure 265A   Figure 265B   Figure 265C

Neckline Dart

This dart can be placed anywhere along the neckline. Its width often takes the form of folds or gathers. In a suit jacket, it is very common for the front shoulder dart to be shifted into the neckline and concealed by the collar.

Draw the new placement line for the dart (in green, Figure 266), then cut to the bust point.

Close up the front shoulder dart with tape: the neckline dart will then open up naturally (Figure 267).

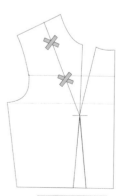

Figure 266   Figure 267

CUT LINES

Placing a cut line on the pattern corresponds to cutting that entire piece of the garment into two pieces, which will then be put back together by an assembly seam. Cut lines are marked on a garment either to respond to a technical necessity or for aesthetic reasons.

Technical Cut Lines

The placement of these cut lines depends on the design being made and the rules for drafting the pattern.

In the case of a flared skirt with a yoke, the cut line must be placed at the upper hip line (10 cm from the waist) to be able to close up the waist darts, which are the same length as the yoke.

If the yoke cutout is placed higher or lower than the upper hip line, it will no longer be possible for all the darts to be absorbed.

Another relevant case is a flared dress with front shoulder cuts. In this kind of design, the cut lines absolutely must pass through the bust points. In this way, the darts are integrated into the cut lines. If the cut line were positioned somewhere else, the dart closure seam would have to be placed right next to the cut line. In that case, the dress would not match the design and the result would not succeed aesthetically.

Aesthetic Cut Lines

Cut lines that are intended to improve the aesthetic effect of a garment can be placed anywhere at all.

Their placement is sometimes dictated by the need to economize on the fabric, and sometimes just as an expression of the designer's creativity: for example, to harmoniously assemble two fabrics of different colors.

Very often, the assembly seam for the cut includes topstitching or a band of fabric integrated between two pattern pieces.

The bib insert shown here as an example (a yoke on the upper part of the bodice of the design, in blue) was created without following any rules of construction. The cut line does not pass through the bust point and does not involve any darts. It is simply a decorative addition to enhance and personalize the design.

MANIPULATING THE SLEEVE

Manipulating the pattern of a straight sleeve is not as complex as manipulating a bodice and does not require you to follow as many rules: you only have to maintain the vertical drape line of the sleeve and the proportions between the sleeve back and front.

For any sleeve design, there is a technique that is both very effective and simple to use: the cutting method.

It involves first drawing the cut lines, separating the cut-out pieces, and then constructing the desired sleeve shape. This method can be applied in three ways:

- Vertical cut: the butterfly sleeve
- Horizontal cut: the balloon sleeve
- Cut along the slope (often called "sunshine" cut): the sleeve with a gathered sleeve cap

In the following pages, you will find some examples of manipulations of the straight-sleeve pattern. They are presented step by step and will allow you to better understand this technique of manipulating through cutting.

BUTTERFLY SLEEVE

Start by carefully analyzing the design to determine how to position the cut lines to obtain the sleeve design presented here.

Because the sleeve cap fits snugly into the armhole, you can change its shape somewhat, but you must not do anything to change its length. The sleeve has a comfortable flare at the bottom, and you can deduce from this that the vertical cut will be the most appropriate to create the butterfly sleeve design.

At approximately regular intervals, draw vertical lines along the width of the bottom of the sleeve (Figure 268 then cut up from the bottom until about 2 mm from the edge of the sleeve cap so that the pieces you have cut out will not become separated.

Spread the parts out at regular intervals to keep the original proportions between the back and the front (Figure 269).

Now redraw the outline of the sleeve, rounding the angles that were created during the manipulation. Do not forget to position the reference notches and assembly notches. Add a 1-cm seam allowance all the way around and mark the hemline length.

This sleeve style has a more attractive drape when it is cut on the bias, so place the straight grain at a 45-degree angle (Figure 270).

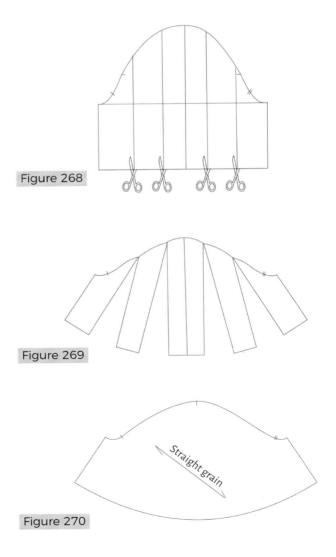

Figure 268

Figure 269

Figure 270

Straight grain

GATHERED SLEEVE CAP

This design, unlike the previous one, involves a gathered sleeve cap and a relatively straight sleeve base.

When you are choosing how to place the cut lines (vertically, horizontally, or in a "sunshine" pattern), think about the shapes. For this sleeve design, you will need to add fullness both in the width (to create the gathers) and in the height (so the gathers will not be flattened but can balloon out).

To observe these two criteria, start by separating the base of the sleeve from the sleeve cap, placing the cut line about 2 cm below the armhole line (Figure 271). The best way to separate the bottom from the sleeve cap to get enough length for the gathers is to use the "sunshine" cut. This is what you will do.

First draw a vertical line, which will indicate both the drape of the sleeve and the distances between the cut-out pieces (red line, Figure 272).

Then separate the pieces in width and in height, first along the side of the sleeve cap. Measure their distances to the red line, and then transfer these measurements to the front side of the sleeve and position the various pieces.

Redraw the outline of the sleeve, position the reference notches and assembly notches, and indicate the straight-grain direction. Then, add the seam allowance and determine the hemline length.

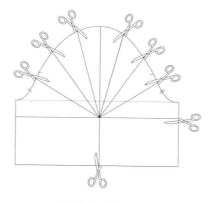

Figure 271

Figure 272

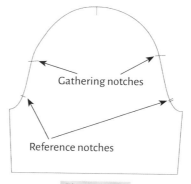

Gathering notches

Reference notches

Figure 273

BALLOON SLEEVE

In this sleeve design, the gathers are present both at the sleeve cap and at the cuff of the sleeve. This means that during the manipulation, you will have to add fullness in both width and height—in other words, in a balanced way across the entire surface of the sleeve. To create this fullness in both directions, the best solution is combining vertical and horizontal cuts.

The first cut line is placed horizontally, about 2 to 3 cm below the armhole line; the next one is placed at the level of the upper chest line. The vertical lines, meanwhile, are placed in the middle of the back and the middle of the front. Cut the vertical and horizontal lines (Figure 274).

On another piece of paper, first draw a vertical line that will indicate the drape line of the manipulated sleeve (in red, Figure 275). Place the two back pieces of the bottom of the sleeve spaced in such a way as to create the desired width. Then, do the same for the other back sleeve pieces, keeping the same spacing for height and width.

Position the front sleeve pieces symmetrically to the back pieces you have just laid out (Figure 275).

Now redraw the outline of the sleeve, mark the reference notches and the assembly notches, indicate the straight grain direction, and add the seam allowance and determine the hem length (Figure 276).

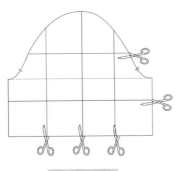

Figure 274

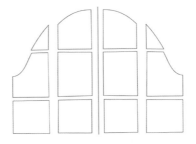

Figure 275

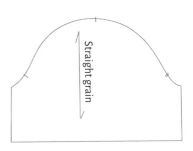

Straight grain

Figure 276

SOME IMPORTANT RECOMMENDATIONS

Here are some useful recommendations to keep in mind for the manipulations of the sleeve:

- The spacing widths and the number of pieces that you cut must absolutely be the same on the back and the front sides of the sleeve so that the original proportions given to the sleeve will be maintained
- The placement of the cut lines and the spacing of the pieces should be done first on one side of the sleeve (for instance, the back side), and then in identical fashion on the other side (in this case, the front)
- Do not place the cut line on the armhole line of the sleeve; if necessary, position it slightly above or below to keep the full shape of the intersection of the armhole curve with the length line
- When reconstituting the sleeve after cutting, always start from the drape line of the sleeve, which is vertical: To do this, take another sheet of paper and first draw a vertical line, then position the cut-out pieces
- Always remember to add more height to the sleeve if the sleeve includes gathers or folds

With the three kinds of cuts (vertical, horizontal, and on the diagonal), you can perform all the imaginable manipulations to produce any kind of sleeve pattern you like, including elaborate designs.

Calculating the Width of the Gathers

Often, when you carry out the necessary manipulation to establish the gathers, you do not really know how widely to space the cut-out pieces to produce the desired gathers. Here is a simple technique for calculating the exact length of the fabric to be gathered.

Take a piece that is 20 cm wide, for example, apply the desired gathers (closer together or farther apart, depending), then measure the width obtained after applying the gathers: in this example, it is 12 cm (Figure 277).

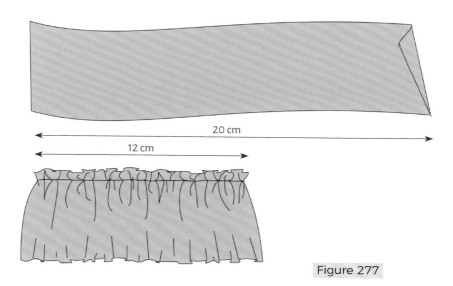

20 cm

12 cm

Figure 277

Now divide the total width of the sleeve by the reference measurement just obtained (12 cm in this case, the width obtained for the gathered piece) to find out how many gathered pieces you will need to reach the total width of the sleeve. *For example, if the total width of the sleeve is 36 cm, we divide that by 12 and get 3: thus, you will need 3 gathered units (Figure 278).*

3 units x 20 cm (ungathered width) = 60 cm. Thus, you need a total width of 60 cm along the bottom of the sleeve for gathering.

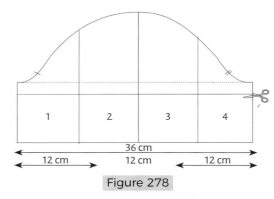

Figure 278

Now add 24 cm to the width along the bottom: 60 cm (total desired width) minus 36 cm (total initial width) = 24 cm.

In the example shown here, three cuts are necessary (between 1 and 2; between 2 and 3; and between 3 and 4, Figure 278).

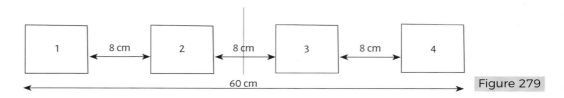

Figure 279

Because you have added 24 cm to the width of the bottom of the sleeve, these will be divided out evenly among the three cuts, making 8 cm (24 divided by 3) between each two pieces (Figure 279).

Pleat Width

The technique used to calculate the exact measurement to be added when applying pleats is a little simpler than the one used for calculating the width of the gathers.

Fold the fabric, or just a piece of paper that has the desired width for the pleats, position the fold notches, then unfold and measure the distance between the notches.

Follow the examples shown here to obtain a 5-cm-wide flat fold, you must add 10 cm (Figure 280A), and to get a 10-cm-wide box pleat, you need to add 20 cm (Figure 280B).

In other words, the width you need to add is always twice the thickness of the fold, whether it is a flat fold or a box pleat.

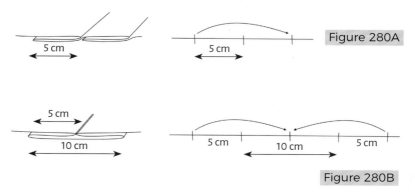

Figure 280A

Figure 280B

In general, when manipulating the pattern of the straight skirt, you will only take the upper hip line and full hip line into account. The upper hip line is used for positioning yokes, pockets, or a lowered waist, for example. The full hip line is used to maintain the original width if the sides are spread out. For the length of the skirt, on the other hand, starting from the full hip line, all kinds of modifications are possible. There is no rule that needs to be adhered to, not even the vertical drape: you can freely express and carry out any ideas that come to your mind, even the most extravagant. However, there are still some elements, explained in the following text, that should be respected to make your manipulation successful.

You will also find some pieces of advice to follow during simple manipulations, which can give you ideas for how to modify the basic skirt pattern into more or less elaborate designs. Nevertheless, just as with the bodice or the sleeve, applying a manipulation assumes that you are following a certain method, and to establish the order of your work, you will first have to analyze the design.

Note

The suggestions given here for manipulating the basic skirt pattern are intended for designs made from fabric in a warp/weft weave, not designs made out of knits or stretchy fabric.

ELIMINATING THE DARTS

You can totally eliminate the waist darts on a skirt— unlike on a bodice, where darts can be shifted, pivoted, added, or moved, but never fully eliminated.

This manipulation, which involves making the waist darts disappear, determines the width of the bottom of the skirt. We say that the skirt is flared by closing the dart at the waist.

Extend the axis of the dart to the bottom of the skirt, cut along the line you have just drawn, and eliminate the width of the dart (Figure 281A). If the basic skirt has two waist darts (page 124), proceed in the same way. Pivot the side part of the skirt (in blue, Figure 281B) by closing the waist dart, which is done by laying the arms of the dart being removed on top of each other.

Now redraw the new shape of the skirt, rounding out the angles that have formed during the manipulation (Figure 281C).

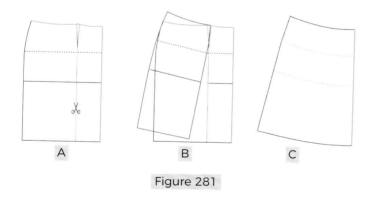

A   B   C

Figure 281

FLARING THE SIDES OF THE SKIRT

In the example of the skirt that is flared by eliminating the darts, the width of the base of the skirt is automatically fixed. This width depends on the widths of the darts: the wider the darts, the wider the skirt.

However, if you want to increase the width of the bottom of the skirt even more, you must not move the side line by more than 4 cm. Otherwise, you will not get a balanced shape all around the skirt: the flare will only happen along the side, and the front part of the skirt will stay perfectly flat (Figure 282).

To give the skirt more flare than can be obtained just by closing up the darts, you will have to apply the cutting method. This manipulation technique allows you to distribute the shapes all around the skirt in a perfectly balanced way (Figure 283).

To do this, draw the cut lines (while taking into account the one that already exists, namely the axis of the dart, Figure 284A), assigning the same width to each piece. Then spread the pieces out, with even spacing in between them, starting with the center front piece (Figure 284B). Finally, redraw the outline of the skirt, rounding out the angles that have formed during the manipulation (Figure 284C).

Figure 282   Figure 283

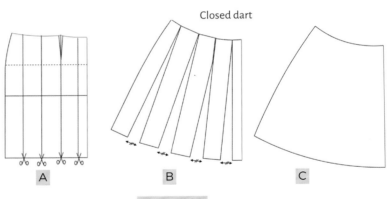

Closed dart

A   B   C

Figure 284

Note

When manipulating a skirt by cutting, it's easier to redraw the skirt outline after spreading out the pieces if you apply several cut lines, because that makes the angles between the spread-out pieces smaller. If there are only a few cut lines, the spread-out pieces will be wider, the angles will be greater, and it will be harder to redraw the original shape, especially at the waistline.

YOKES

As you saw earlier, the upper part of the skirt, and more particularly the upper hip line, plays an important role in manipulating the basic skirt pattern. This line, which plays no part in the construction of the basic pattern (page 36), is essential here for manipulation.

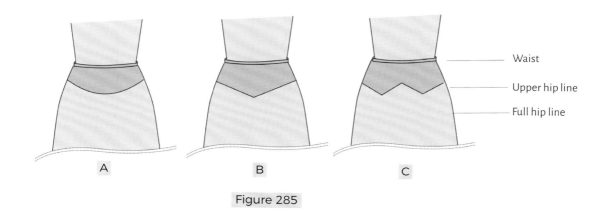

Figure 285

At the level of the upper hips, position the pockets (for greater comfort) and any kinds of yokes or inserts (Figures 285A, B, and C) added for aesthetic or technical reasons (for instance to close the waist darts).

Often, to eliminate the back waist darts, they are placed inside the cut line (in green, Figure 286). It is important to know that this horizontal displacement of the darts can be applied on the skirt back but **never** on the skirt front.

To eliminate the darts on the front of the upper part of the skirt, you must first close them by flaring the skirt, and then draw the cut line (in green, Figure 287).

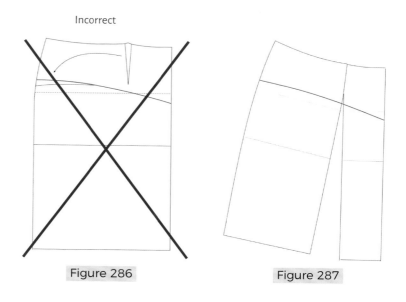

Incorrect

Figure 286

Figure 287

MANIPULATING THE PANTS

Manipulating the basic pants pattern involves following two rules:

- Never modify the crotch curve
- Maintain the original proportions of the leg widths

As with the manipulations applied to the skirt, the bodice, and the sleeve, one of the best methods to use is cutting.

In general, manipulating pants means either widening or narrowing them, either at the top or at the bottom.

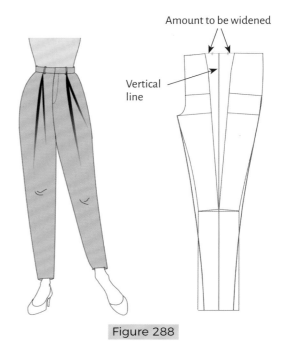

Figure 288

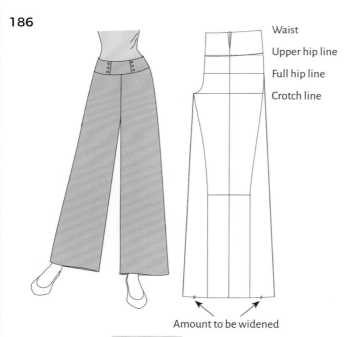

Amount to be widened

Figure 289

When you widen the top of the pants, you will often use pleats at the waist. In this kind of modification, the first cut line is drawn at the level of the knees, and then along the line of the central crease.

To maintain the proportions, the widening of the upper part is done in a way that is balanced on either side of the central crease (Figure 288). Then, on the lower part of the pants, the outer flare lines are extended to meet those below the knee, depending on the pants design (the width at the bottom).

Widening the lower part of the pants is much simpler: starting at the front crotch, draw a straight line to the already existing line of the bottom of the pants, closer to or farther from the central crease line depending on how much you want to widen it by. Then, on the back side, starting at an equal distance from the central crease line along the floor, draw a straight line up to the full hip line (in green, Figure 289).

A low-waisted pants design is manipulated the same way as a skirt.

PATTERN-MAKING TOOLS

There are many accessories that are useful to varying degrees for drawing patterns. Here is a list of the essential tools.

Paper for drawing the patterns on. You can draw the patterns on any kind of paper as long as it has a smooth surface and a solid color and is resistant and reasonably thick (90 to 100 g/cm2) and at least 70 x 70cm in size. One of the most suitable kinds of paper for patternmaking is Kraft paper, sold in rolls or large sheets.

A **tape measure** for taking body measurements.

A **pencil** for drawing the construction lines of the pattern. Choose a pencil with a lead that is not too hard, so that you can erase easily if necessary. A 2B pencil, for example, works well.

Colored pencils to distinguish the lines of a modification on the basic pattern: ideally blue, green, and red.

 A **ruler**, a **French curve**, and an **L-square** to draw curved, straight, or parallel lines. For the ruler, I recommend that you use a flexible, see-through ruler.

Tracing paper or **carbon paper**, and a **tracing wheel**: you must absolutely make sure to have these so that you can copy the pattern elements after the manipulation.

A **marker**, a piece of **chalk**, or a **fabric pencil** for drawing the lines on the fabric precisely. The quality of the fabric will determine which of these tools you should choose: For a smooth, fine fabric, you can use chalk, but for a thick, soft fabric the pencil will work better.

Two **pairs of scissors**, one for cutting the paper and the other for cutting the fabric. Whatever you do, do not substitute either of these for the other; each one has its own specific use.

 Notching pliers for making the reference notches and assembly notches on the pattern.

Thread clippers, very useful for cutting threads.

 Long, thin **pins**—the easiest kind to use.

INDEX